Contents

D0841466

© 1997 Abingdon Press.

Illustrated by:

• Robert S. Jones

Contributing Writers:

• Sharilyn S. Adair
• Elizabeth Crocker
• Daphna Flegal
• Susan Isbell
• Joyce Riffe
• LeeDell Stickler

Baptism & Communion

Supplies

- Bible
- CD player
- CD
- crayons, markers, pencils
- glue, clear tape, masking tape, tacks
- stapler, staples
- construction paper
- colored cellophane
- blue crepe paper
- colored tissue paper strips
- plain paper
- watercolor paint sets
- watercolor brushes
- tempera paint
- scissors
- plastic tablecloths or beach towels
- paper punch
- yarn
- smocks or aprons
- towels
- plastic dishpan, tub, or bowl
- plastic containers
- newspapers
- large and small paper bags

- paper towels
- coffee filters
- glitter or glitter glue
- box lids, trays, shallow trays
- Communion items
- craft sticks or tongue depressors
- cleanup supplies
- white feathers
- four sponges
- Communion cups
- plastic grapes
- white felt
- purple felt
- plastic dove
- quilt, pillows, or rocking chair
- dolls or doll clothes
- egg cartons
- clothespins or paper clips
- clothesline, string, or drying rack
- baking sheets
- large plastic pitcher or container
- paper plates
- paper cups
- plastic cups

- measuring cups and spoons
- small plastic pitcher
- platters
- cooking utensils
- napkins
- bread basket
- different kinds of bread
- cookie dough, flour, rolling pins, cookie sheets
- bottle of grape juice
- water
- pretzels, crackers
- cheese, grapes, dates, figs or fig cookies, olives, pomegranates
- canned or frozen bread dough, or ingredients for bread dough
- honey, butter
- powdered drink mix
- carrot sticks
- food coloring

Scriptures for Baptism

Matthew 3:13-17; Mark 1:9-11; Luke 3:21-22; John 1:29-34

Understanding the Bible Verses

John, often known as John the Baptist, was the son of Elizabeth and Zechariah. He was a relative of Jesus and probably had known Jesus all his life. The ministry of John the Baptist set the stage for the baptism of Jesus. John had become a charismatic preacher, working in the Judean wilderness. He preached repentance and baptized people with water as a sign of forgiveness. The symbolic cleansing by water helped the people understand that God had washed away their old sinful lives.

Jesus came to John as one of the crowd, as one of those who was coming to God. While Jesus did not need to confess sins in order to be baptized, his submission to the same baptism as those around him symbolized the beginning of his public ministry, and also identified him closely with those he came to save.

The dove is symbolic of the Holy Spirit. It is significant to our understanding of the sacrament because it shows that baptism is not merely an action on our part. It is important to remember that God is the primary actor in the sacrament of baptism. Baptism is a time when we receive the Holy Spirit as we are claimed by God.

Understanding Your Children

Young children may not be able to grasp fully the significance of baptism, but they can recognize that baptism is important to people in the church. Some children may have seen babies baptized in the worship service of their churches or may have seen photographs of their own baptisms. For other children these lessons may be their first introduction to the sacrament of baptism.

It is important for all children, whether or not they have been baptized, to know that God loves them, that they are children of God, and that they belong to God. Baptism is one way that we recognize and celebrate that we belong to God.

Water is an important element in these lessons on baptism. Young children are sensory learners. They can connect with the sound and feel of water. Help them recognize ways that water is used and is important to each of us. Then help your children discover that baptizing with water is one special way that the church uses water.

One way children experience the love of God is through the church family. You are the church for the children you teach. You are also direct evidence of the church's intention to keep the promise of nurture made at infant baptisms. In a very real sense baptism teaches children that they are part of the family of God.

Developing Your Faith

Read Matthew 3:13-17; Mark 1:9-11; Luke 3:21-22; and John 1:29-34. Compare the stories of Jesus' baptism as they are written in the four Gospels. The Matthew, Mark, and Luke verses all testify that Jesus is God's beloved son. Through Jesus you are a beloved child of God. God is well-pleased with you, not because of anything you have done or have not done, but because you are simply you.

Read Matthew 3:13-17. Water is a life-giving symbol when it is used in baptism. Remember your baptism and the promises that were made when you were publicly identified as a child of God. If you have a hymnal available, read the ritual for baptism. How is God calling you to live out your baptism?

Read Mark 1:9-11. When Jesus was baptized, he was empowered by the Holy Spirit to begin his ministry. Do you see evidence of the Holy Spirit at work in your life? Pray that the Holy Spirit will empower you in your ministry with children. Pray for each of your children by name.

Baptism

God said, "You are my own dear Son. I am pleased with you."

(Mark 1:11, *Good News Bible*, adapted)

Lesson Overview

✓ Learning Experiences	✓ Supplies	✓ Before Class
Who's Who	CD, CD player, nametags *(page 29)*, blue crayons, marker, paper punch, scissors, yarn or tape	Photocopy and cut out nametags.
Touch the Water	plastic tablecloths, dishpans, water, paper cups, smocks, bowls, towels, doll clothes or plastic dolls, sponges, clothesline and clothespins or drying rack, tray, plastic pitcher	
Clean Up	CD, CD player, towels, *page 72*	
Water World Warbles	none	
Touch 'n Tell Bible Story	"A Special Child of God" *(page 5)*, towels, plastic tablecloth, plastic tub or bowl, water, plastic pitcher	
Bible Verse Round	CD; CD player; Bible; plastic dove or dove outline (page 18); cardboard, scissors	Photocopy page 18.
Splash 'n Sing	CD, CD player, *page 38*	
Window Wonders	colored cellophane, story window (page 10), scissors, glue, tape, crayons	Photocopy story window.
Clean Up	CD, CD player, *page 72*	
Ring Around a Verse	none	
Share a Salty Snack	plastic pitcher, salty pretzels or crackers, napkins, paper cups, water	
Time to Go	window wonders, parent's page *(page 9)*	Photocopy parent's page.

A Special Child of God

by Susan Isbell

Trickle trickle, drip drop, splish splash, plip plop!

The water of the river made swishy sounds as it lapped at the sandy bank. Jesus took off his sandals and waded out into the water.

Trickle trickle, drip drop, splish splash, plip plop!

The cool water felt good as it swirled around Jesus' ankles, then up to his knees.

Jesus walked to meet John, who was already in the river.

Trickle trickle, drip drop, splish splash, plip plop!

The water dripped through John's fingers and ran along his arms.

"I have come to be baptized," Jesus said. "I know that God loves me. If you baptize me, everyone will know that I belong to God."

Trickle trickle, drip drop, splish splash, plip plop!

The water splashed over Jesus' head and ran down his hair and onto his back. The water felt good. The water felt clean.

Trickle trickle, drip drop, splish splash, plip plop!

Jesus shook the water from his hair and looked up. In the sky he saw a dove.

Jesus heard a voice say, "You are my own dear Son. I am pleased with you." Jesus knew the voice was the voice of God.

Trickle trickle, drip drop, splish splash, plip plop!

Jesus climbed out of the water. Jesus knew that God loved him. Jesus knew that he belonged to God.

(*Based on Mark 1:9-11*)

Copyright © 1996, 1998 Cokesbury

From *Touch the Water, Taste the Bread, Ages 3–5.* © 1998 Cokesbury. Art © 1997 Abingdon Press. Reprinted by permission.

Who's Who

CD, CD player, nametags (*page 29*), blue crayons, marker, paper punch, scissors, yarn or tape

- Play "Water Sounds" from the **CD** as the children arrive. Greet each child by name. If you do not know the children's names, make nametags.

- Copy and cut out the nametags with the water pictures (*page 29*). Make one nametag for each child. Let the child color the nametag with blue crayons. Write the child's name on the nametag with a marker. Use a paper punch to make a hole in the top of the nametag. Measure a length of yarn to fit over the child's head. Thread the yarn through the hole and tie the ends together to make a nametag necklace. Or tape the nametag to the child's clothing.

- **Say: The picture on our nametags makes me think about water. Listen to the sounds playing in our room. What do you hear? I hear water running over the rocks in a river. Water is very important in our world. Can you think of a way we use water?**

- Talk with the children about the different ways we use water, such as washing dishes, washing clothes, drinking, watering plants, bathing, and cooking.

- **Say: Water is used for something very special in the church. It is used for baptism. Our Bible story is when Jesus was baptized with water.**

Touch the Water

plastic tablecloths, dishpans, water, paper cups, smocks, bowls, towels, doll clothes or plastic dolls, sponges, clothesline and clothespins or drying rack, tray, plastic pitcher

- Set up two to four areas for the children to experience different activities with water. Choose the activities that fit your particular group of children and your room arrangement. Let the children move from activity to activity as they show interest.

Water Play

- Cover the table or floor with a plastic tablecloth. Place one or two dishpans partially filled with water on the plastic cloth. Add bowls and paper cups. Have the children wear smocks to protect their clothing. Have towels on hand to dry hands and arms.

- Encourage the children to pour, dip, and experience the water. Have the children listen to the water as they pour it from the cups and bowls.

Sponge Play

- Cover the table or floor with a plastic tablecloth. Set a plastic dishpan partially filled with water on the cloth. Give the children sponges. Show the children how the sponges will float on the water. Show the children how to dip the sponges into a dishpan of water and then squeeze the excess water out of the sponges. Have the children use the wet sponges to wash the tables and chairs.

Wash Doll Clothes or Dolls

- Cover the table or floor with a plastic tablecloth. Set a plastic dishpan partially filled with water on the cloth. Let the children wash doll clothes or plastic dolls. Have a clothesline and clothespins or drying rack on hand for doll clothes.

Drink Water

- Use a plastic pitcher filled with water, a tray, and paper cups. Set the paper cups on the tray. Let each child pour water from the pitcher into a paper cup. The tray will help contain any spills. Let the children drink the water from the cup.

Talk About the Experiences

- Talk about how the water feels. Guide the children in thinking about the different ways we use water, such as washing dishes, washing clothes, drinking, watering plants, bathing, and cooking.

- **Say: Water is important in our world. It is used for drinking and helping plants grow. Water is used to help make things clean. Water is used for something very special in the church. It is used for baptism. Our Bible story is about the time when Jesus was baptized with water.**

Clean Up

CD, CD player, towels, *page 72*

- Allow fifteen to twenty minutes for the "Who's Who" and the "Touch the Water" activities, then have the children help clean up. Play "The Cleanup Song" (*page 72*) from the **CD** to signal cleanup time. Encourage all the children to participate. Have towels available to dry hands and arms and to mop up spills.

Water World Warbles

none

- Invite the children to join you in your story area.

- **Say: Water is very important in our world. God planned for water to help things grow and live. God planned for water to help make things clean.**

- Sing the words printed below to the tune of "This Is the Way." Have the children do the motions.

> God planned for water in our world,
> In our world, in our world.
> God planned for water in our world,
> So we can brush our teeth. (*Pretend to brush teeth.*)

© 1996 Cokesbury.

Sing about other ways we use water by changing the last stanza. Let the children make up other stanzas.

> **So we can take a bath.** (*Pretend to wash arms and legs.*)
> **So we can splash and swim.** (*Pretend to swim.*)
> **So we can wash our face.** (*Pretend to wash face.*)
> **So we can have a drink.** (*Pretend to drink cup of water.*)

- **Say: Water is also important in our church. We use water in our church for baptism.**

- Finish singing the song with a stanza about baptism:

> **So we can be baptized.** (*Touch hand to forehead.*)

Touch 'n Tell Bible Story

"A Special Child of God" (*page 5*), towels, plastic tablecloth, plastic tub or bowl, water, plastic pitcher

- Place a towel or plastic tablecloth in your story area. Set a tub or bowl on the towel or plastic. Make sure the children can see the bowl or tub and that it is placed where you can reach it. Fill the plastic pitcher with water.

- **Say: Our Bible story today is about the time when Jesus was baptized with water in a river.**

- Pour some water from the pitcher into the tub or bowl. Set the pitcher down beside the tub or bowl.

- Use the story "A Special Child of God" (*page 5*) to tell the children the story of Jesus' baptism.

- **Say: Jesus knew that he was God's son and that God loved him. We know that God loves us.**

- Pour more water in the tub or bowl. Have each child come separately to dip his or her hands in the water.

- As each child places his or her hands in the water, **say: You are a child of God. God loves you.**

- Have the children dry their hands on a towel.

Bible Verse Round

CD; CD player; Bible; plastic dove or dove outline (*page 18*), cardboard, scissors

- Have the children sit in a circle on the floor. Choose a child to hold the Bible open to Mark 1:11.

- **Say: Jesus saw a dove when he was baptized. When Jesus saw the dove, he heard God's voice. "God said, 'You are my own dear Son. I am pleased with you'"** (Mark 1:11, *Good News Bible*, adapted).

- Have the children repeat the verse. Show the children the plastic dove. Or photocopy page 18; use the outline as a pattern to cut a dove out of cardboard.

- Play "Water Sounds" from the **CD**. As the children listen to the sounds, have the children pass the dove around the circle. Stop the music.

- Have the child holding the dove when you stopped the music stand up. Have the child hold the dove above his or her head. Have the child sit down. Play "Water Sounds" again and have the children start passing the dove around the circle. Continue the game until every child has repeated the Bible verse.

Splash 'n Sing

CD, CD player, *page 38*

* Sing "Drip, Drop, Splish, Splash" (*page 38*) from the CD. Encourage the children to sing the words to the song with you as they move to the music.

> Drip, drop,
> (*Clap hands.*)
> Splish, splash,
> (*Pat knees.*)
> Trickle, trickle,
> (*Wiggle fingers.*)
> Flow.
> (*Make a sweeping motion with arms.*)

Words and music by James Ritchie; © 1996 by James Ritchie.

Window Wonders

colored cellophane, story window (*page 10*), scissors, glue, tape, crayons

- Photocopy the story window (*page 10*) for each child. Let the children color the picture with crayons. Remember that young children are developing fine motor skills and may not color within the lines. Affirm the children's work.

- Talk with the children about the picture. Remind the children that John baptized Jesus with water.

- Cut colored cellophane sheets into small pieces and place them on the work table.

- **Say: Some church windows have colored glass. The colored glass makes pictures that tell Bible stories. Let's pretend that the colored cellophane is glass for church windows. Let's make our pictures into church windows that tell the Bible story of Jesus' baptism.**

- Have the children glue the colored cellophane pieces all over their pictures.

- Hold the children's pictures up to the light or tape the pictures to a window. Point out how the light shines through the colors.

Clean Up

CD, CD player, *page 72*

- Play "The Cleanup Song" (*page 72*) to signal cleanup time again. Have the children help pick up paper scraps and put away crayons and glue.

- Plan easy-to-cleanup activities at the close of the lesson to keep children involved while they wait for parents. If children are busy, they will be less likely to become anxious if other parents arrive first.

Ring Around a Verse

- Choose a child to hold hands with you to make a bridge (like the game London Bridge). Have the children stand in a line ready to go under the bridge. Sing the song below to the tune of "London Bridge." Have the children march under the bridge while you sing. On the line, "I am pleased with you," bring the arms of the bridge down to catch the child under the bridge. Repeat until each child has been caught.

  God said, "You are my dear son,
      My dear son, my dear son."
  God said, "You are my dear son.
      I am pleased with you."

- **Pray: Thank you, God, for Jesus. Thank you for water. Thank you for each of us. We are your children. Amen.**

Share a Salty Snack

plastic pitcher, salty pretzels or crackers, napkins, paper cups, water

- Choose children to hand out napkins and paper cups. Serve a salty snack such as pretzels or crackers. Let the children pour water to drink from the plastic pitcher. Talk about how the water tastes good and refreshing after eating something salty. Remind the children that water is important in our world.

- **Pray: Thank you, God, for water to drink. Amen.**

Time to Go

window wonders, parent's page (*page 9*)

- Give the children the window wonders to take home. Give parents the parent's page (*page 9*) and encourage them to talk about water and baptism at home. Tell parents about any additional lessons you have planned as part of this study. Encourage parents to take their children to worship when a baptism will take place.

Parent's Page

Baptism is an important sacrament in the church.

Baptism is one way we publicly acknowledge God's claim on us and recognize God's love for us. Today's lesson on baptism introduced your child to the sacrament and to the Bible story about Jesus' baptism.

Just as Jesus' baptism showed that he belonged to God and that God was with him, baptism in the church today shows that God loves us and that we belong to God's family.

Look at the Bible

Open your family's Bible to Mark 1:9-11. Show the page to your child.

Say: The Bible tells us the story about the time when Jesus was baptized with water. When Jesus was baptized, "God said, 'You are my own dear Son. I am pleased with you'" (Mark 1:11, *Good News Bible*, adapted).

Remind your child that God loves each of us and that we all belong to God. Each of us is a child of God.

Touch the Water

Partially fill a plastic tub or sink with water. Add small floating toys, sponges, plastic cups, and bowls. Let your child enjoy playing in the water.

Let your child enjoy outside water play, if weather permits. Let your child play in water from a sprinkler or hose. Or fill a bucket with water, give your child a paintbrush, and let your child paint a fence or the sidewalk with water.

Talk about how important water is to your family. Remind your child that you drink water and use water to take a bath, to brush your teeth, and to wash your clothes. Tell your child that water is used in a special way in the church. Water is used for baptism.

Sing-a-Verse

Sing the Bible verse with your child. Sing the song printed below to the tune of "London Bridge."

> God said, "You are my dear son,
>   My dear son, my dear son."
> God said, "You are my dear son.
>   I am pleased with you."

Parent's Page

Parent's Page

Baptism

God said, "You are my own dear Son. I am pleased with you."

(Mark 1:11, *Good News Bible*, adapted)

Lesson Overview

✔ Learning Experiences	✔ Supplies	✔ Before Class
Who's Who	CD, CD player, nametags *(page 29)*, blue crayons, marker, paper punch, scissors, yarn or tape	Photocopy and cut out nametags.
Touch the Water	sponges, plastic tablecloths, dishpans, water, paper cups, smocks, towels	
Water Waves	blue crepe paper streamers, blue or white construction paper, crayons, tape or glue	Cut construction paper in half lengthwise for each child.
Clean Up	CD, CD player, towels, *page 72*	
Water Dance	CD, CD player, water streamers	
Move 'n Tell Bible Story	water streamers, *page 12*	
Bible Verse Round	CD; CD player; Bible; plastic dove or dove pattern *(page 18)*; cardboard; scissors	
Splash 'n Sing	CD, CD player, *page 38*	
Baptism Banners	paintbrushes, baptism banner *(page 18)*, watercolor paint sets, plastic containers, water, newspapers, smocks	Photocopy baptism banner for each child.
Clean Up	CD, CD player, *page 72*	
Visit the Baptismal Font	baptismal font, Baptism Today picture cards *(page 19)*, scissors, construction paper, glue or tape	
Share a Snack	napkins, tray, paper cups, water, powdered drink mix, carrot sticks, large pitcher or container, small plastic pitcher	
Water Games	paper cups, water, bucket or tub, towels, plastic tablecloths	
Time to Go	baptism banners, parent's page *(page 17)*	Photocopy parent's page.

JESUS Is Baptized by Susan Isbell

The *water* of the river made swishy sounds as it lapped at the sandy bank.

Some parts of the river were very deep, and the *water* was very still. Other parts of the river were very shallow, and the *water* flowed over the rocks. People with bare feet waded into the shallow *water*.

In one part of the river a man named John stood in the *water*. John was baptizing people with *water*. As the people felt the *water* run over their heads, John would tell them to live the way God wanted them to live.

One day Jesus came to the river. Jesus waded out into the *water* of the river.

As Jesus came out of the *water*, a dove flew down from the clouds. Jesus heard God's voice. "You are my own dear Son, and I am pleased with you," God said. Jesus felt the cool *water* of the river swirling around him. He knew he belonged to God.

(*Based on Mark 1:9-11.*)

Who's Who

 CD, CD player, nametags (*page 29*), blue crayons, marker, paper punch, scissors, yarn or tape

- Play "Water Sounds" on the **CD** as the children arrive. Greet each child by name. If you do not know the children's names, use nametags (*page 29*) again this week. Have nametags (*page 6*) available for children who were not present for the first session.

- As you give each child his or her nametag, **say: The picture on our nametags makes me think about water. Listen to the sounds playing in our room. What do you hear? I hear sounds of water running over the rocks in a river. Water is very important in our world. Can you think of a way we use water?**

- Remind the children about the different ways we use water, such as washing dishes, washing clothes, drinking, watering plants, bathing, and cooking.

- **Say: Water is used for something very special in the church. It is used for baptism. Our Bible story today is about the time when Jesus was baptized with water.**

Touch the Water

 sponges, plastic tablecloths, dishpans, water, paper cups, smocks, towels

Cover the table or floor with a plastic tablecloth. Place one or two dishpans partially filled with water on the plastic cloth. Add the paper cups and sponges. Have the children wear smocks. Have towels available to dry hands and arms.

- Encourage the children to experience the water. Show the children how to dip the sponges into the water and then squeeze the excess water out of the sponges. Have the children use the wet sponges to wash the tables and chairs.

- Talk about how the water feels. Guide the children in thinking about the different ways we use water, such as washing dishes, washing clothes, drinking, watering plants, bathing, and cooking.

- **Say: Water is important in our world. Water is used for drinking and for helping plants grow. Water is used to help make things clean. Water is used for something very special in the church. It is used for baptism. Our Bible story is about the time when Jesus was baptized with water.**

Water Waves

 blue crepe paper streamers, blue or white construction paper, crayons, tape or glue

- Cut a piece of blue or white construction paper in half lengthwise for each child. Give each child both halves of the paper. Write the children's names on their papers.

- Let the children decorate the papers with crayons.

- Help the children roll each half of the papers into tubes. Tape the sides of the tubes together.

- Give each child three or four blue crepe paper streamers. Help the children glue or tape the streamers around each tube.

- Show the children how to put the tubes over their wrists like bracelets.

- Talk with the children about ways we use water. Tell the children that they can pretend their streamers are waves of water. When they wave their arms, the water will move. Encourage the children to wave their arms in big, sweeping motions to make large waves. Encourage the children to make small circle motions to make ripples of water.

- **Say: Water is important in our world. Water is used for drinking and for helping plants grow. Water is used to help make things clean. Water is used for something very special in the church. It is used for baptism. Our Bible story is about the time when Jesus was baptized with water.**

Clean Up

CD, CD player, towels, *page 72*

- Play The Cleanup Song" (*page 72*) on the **CD** to signal cleanup time. Encourage all the children to participate. Have towels available to dry hands and arms and to mop up spills.

Water Dance

CD, CD player, water streamers

- Invite the children to bring their water streamers and to join you in an open area of the room.

- Play "Water Sounds" from the **CD**.

- Say the following poem for the children in a loud voice. Encourage the children to wave their streamers with big, sweeping movements.

  Splash! Crash! Splash!
  Hear the water sounds.
  Splash! Crash! Splash!
  The water's rushing all around.

- Lower the volume on the **CD**. Say the next lines of the poem in a normal voice. Encourage the children to move like raindrops.

  Drip! Drop! Drip!
  Hear the water sounds.
  Drip! Drop! Drip!
  The water's dripping down, down, down.

- Lower the volume on the CD still more. Say the last lines of the poem in a whisper. Have the children move more slowly and gently.

  Splisssh, wusssh, splisssh.
  Hear the water sounds.
  Splisssh, wusssh, splisssh.
  Water's swirling 'round and 'round.

- Softly tell the children to hold their water streamers very still and to sit down in the story area.

Move 'n Tell Bible Story

water streamers, *page 12*

- **Say: Our Bible story today is about the time when Jesus was baptized with water in a river. I want you to help me tell the Bible story. Every time I say the word *water*, I want you to move your water streamers like waves of water.**

- Tell the story "Jesus Is Baptized" (*page 12*). Emphasize the word *water* each time it appears. After the story, collect the water streamers from the children.

Bible Verse Round

CD; CD player; Bible; plastic dove or dove pattern (*page 18*), cardboard, and scissors

- Have the children sit in a circle on the floor. Choose a child to hold the Bible open to Mark 1:11.

- **Say: Jesus saw a dove when he was baptized in the river. When Jesus saw the dove, he heard God's voice. "God said, 'You are my own dear Son. I am pleased with you'" (Mark 1:11, *Good News Bible*, adapted).**

- Have the children repeat the verse with you. Show the children the plastic dove. Or using the dove pattern on page 18, cut a dove out of cardboard.

- Play "Water Sounds" from the **CD**. As the children listen to the sounds, have them pass the dove around the circle. Stop the music.

- Have the child holding the dove when you stopped the music stand up. Have the child hold the dove above his or her head. Say the Bible verse for the child. Have the child repeat the Bible verse after you.

- Have the child sit down. Play "Water Sounds" again and have the children start passing the dove around the circle. Continue the game until every child has repeated the Bible verse.

Splash 'n Sing

CD, CD player, *page 38*

- Sing the song "Drip, Drop, Splish, Splash" (*page 38*) on the **CD**. Encourage the children to sing the words to the song with you as they move to the music.

Drip, drop,
(*Clap hands.*)
Splish, splash,
(*Pat knees.*)
Trickle, trickle,
(*Wiggle fingers.*)
Flow.
(*Make a sweeping motion with arms.*)

Words and music by James Ritchie; © 1996 James Ritchie.

Baptism Banners

paintbrushes, baptism banner (*page 18*), watercolor paint sets, plastic containers, water, newspapers, smocks

- Photocopy the baptism banner (*page 18*) for each child.

- Cover the table with newspaper. Have the children wear paint smocks.

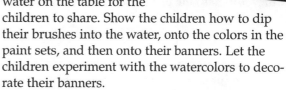

- Give each child a paintbrush. Have the children share watercolor paint sets.

- Set several plastic containers partially filled with water on the table for the children to share. Show the children how to dip their brushes into the water, onto the colors in the paint sets, and then onto their banners. Let the children experiment with the watercolors to decorate their banners.

- **Say: We are using water to mix with our paints to make banners. We use water for something very special in the church. We use water for baptism. Our Bible story today was about a time when Jesus was baptized with water. The dove reminds us of the words God said about Jesus: "You are my own dear Son. I am pleased with you" (Mark 1:11, *Good News Bible*, adapted).**

- Have the children repeat the Bible verse once again. Write each child's name in the space provided on the banner.

- **Say: (*Child's name*) is a child of God.**

- Set the banners aside to dry.

Clean Up

CD, CD player, *page 72*

- Play "The Cleanup Song" (*page 72*) on the **CD** to signal cleanup time once again. Have the children help clean brushes and put away paint sets.

Visit the Baptismal Font

baptismal font, Baptism Today picture cards (*page 19*), scissors, construction paper, glue or tape

- Take the children to the sanctuary to see where people in your church are baptized. Make sure there is water in the baptismal font before taking the children to visit.

- Dip your hand in the water of the font and let the water drip from your fingers back into the font.

- **Say: Water is used for baptism in our church. When someone is baptized, it is a special time. We are saying God loves the person being baptized. And all the people in the church are saying that they will help the person learn more about Jesus and about God. Baptism is a sign that we belong to God and are a part of God's people, the church.**

- Cut apart the Baptism Today picture cards (*page 19*). Mount each picture on a piece of construction paper with glue or tape. Show the children all the cards. Then hold up the picture card that shows one of the ways your church baptizes.

- **Say: This picture reminds me of the way our church baptizes people (babies).**

- Ask your pastor to meet with you and the children to briefly talk about baptism.

- Let the children kneel where people are baptized.

Share a Snack

napkins, tray, paper cups, water, powdered drink mix, carrot sticks, large pitcher or container, small plastic pitcher

- Plan easy-to-cleanup activities at the end of the lesson to keep children busy until parents arrive.

- Let the children help mix water with a powdered drink mix in a large pitcher or container. Pour the drink into the small plastic pitcher. Set paper cups on a tray. Let the children pour the drink into the cups. The tray will help contain spills.

- Choose children to hand out napkins and carrot sticks. Remind the children that water helps carrots and other plants to grow.

- **Pray: Thank you, God, for water. Amen.**

Water Games

paper cups, water, bucket or tub, towels, plastic tablecloths

- Make a path with a plastic tablecloth. Have the children stand in a line on the tablecloth. Have a bucket or tub at the end of the line. If you have a large group of children, have more than one line, tablecloth, and bucket or tub.

- **Say: Water is important to our world. We use water for drinking, for washing, and for helping plants grow. Water is used for something special in the church. It is used for baptism. Baptism reminds us that God loves us and that we are children of God. Let's plan a game with cups of water.**

- Give the first child in line a cup of water. Instruct the children to carefully pass the water from one child to the next. Have the last child in line pour the cup of water into the bucket.

- As the child is pouring the water, **say: God loves (*child's name*). (*Child's name*) is a child of God.**

- Have the child tiptoe (be careful of wet floors) to the front of the line. Play the game until each child has a turn pouring water into the bucket and moving to the front of the line. Use towels to wipe up spills.

Time to Go

baptism banners, parent's page (*page 17*)

- Give the children their baptism banners. Photocopy the parent's page (*page 17*) for each family. If you are offering the "Children and Parents Learning Together About Baptism" lesson, copy the note on page 37 to give to parents.

- Encourage parents to take their children to worship when a baptism will take place.

Parent's Page

Water Wigglers

Enjoy making and eating blue gelatin with your child. Point out that you are using water to make the gelatin. When the gelatin is ready to eat, talk with your child about how the gelatin looks and tastes. Talk about how the gelatin feels wet when you eat it. Tell your child that the blue color of the gelatin reminds you of the blue color of water.

Bubble Fun

Let your child help you mix together ¼ cup liquid detergent, ½ cup water, and 1 teaspoon sugar in a plastic tub or shallow bowl. Tear out the bottoms of paper cups. Show your child how to dip the rims of the cups into the bubble solution and blow through the bottoms. Enjoy watching the bubbles.

Talk with your child about the many ways we use water. Remind your child that one special way the church uses water is in baptism.

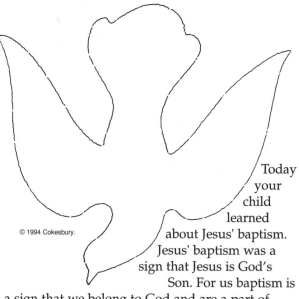

© 1994 Cokesbury.

Today your child learned about Jesus' baptism. Jesus' baptism was a sign that Jesus is God's Son. For us baptism is a sign that we belong to God and are a part of God's people, the church.

If your child has been baptized, share your memories of that experience with your child. Show your child pictures or a baptismal gown, if you have them available. Continue to help your child remember his or her baptism each year on the anniversary of your child's baptism.

Look at the Bible

Open your family's Bible to Mark 1:9-11. Show the page to your child.

Say: The Bible tells us the story about the time when Jesus was baptized with water. When Jesus was baptized, "God said, "You are my own dear Son. I am pleased with you'" (Mark 1:11, *Good News Bible*, adapted).

Remind your child that God loves each of us and that we all belong to God. Each of us is a child of God.

Parent's Page

is a Child of God

Baptism Banner

Baptism Today Picture Cards

19

Baptism

God said, "You are my own dear Son. I am pleased with you."

(Mark 1:11, *Good News Bible*, adapted)

Lesson Overview

✓ Learning Experiences	✓ Supplies	✓ Before Class
Meet 'n Greet	CD, CD player	
Who's Who Station	see page 23	Photocopy and cut out nametags. Photocopy and display directions.
Storybook Station	see page 23	Photocopy and display station directions.
Mix 'n Match Station	see page 23	Photocopy and display station directions.
Touch the Water Station	see page 23	Photocopy and display station directions.
Drip 'n Drop Station	see page 24	Photocopy and display station directions.
Dove Derbies Station	see page 24	Photocopy derbies. Photocopy and display station directions.
Doves in Flight Station	see page 24	Photocopy and cut out dove pattern. Photocopy and display station directions.
Water Wash Station	see page 24	Photocopy and display station directions.
Dove Delights Station	see page 25	Photocopy and display station directions.
Clean Up	CD, CD player, towels, *page 72*	
Sing a Verse	none	
Stand 'n Tell Bible Story	"God's Own Dear Son" (*page 22*), dove derbies	
Bible Verse Round	plastic dove or dove cut from cardboard, CD, CD player, Bible	
Splash 'n Sing	CD, CD player, page 38	
Visit the Baptismal Font	name bags	

Parents and Children Learning Together About Baptism

The lesson "Parents and Children Learning Together About Baptism" is designed for parents and young children to interact with one another. This will provide opportunities for parents and children to explore and to experience together these important sacraments in ways that are appealing and meaningful to young children. Use the lesson as part of a three-lesson series on baptism, as part of a six-lesson series on the sacraments, or as a stand-alone lesson on baptism.

Suggested Schedule (45 minutes to 1½ hours)

Do-Together Stations

(20-30 minutes)
Set up several Do-Together Stations for parents and children to explore. Choose the number of stations based on your room space and the number of people you will have present. If your classroom does not seem big enough, consider moving this lesson to your fellowship hall. Or move quiet activities into a hallway. You also may want to use the kitchen for activities involving food preparation.

Photocopy the directions (pages 28-36) for each station and display the directions in the stations.

Explain to parents that they are to stay with their children and to explore the Do-Together Stations for the next twenty to thirty minutes. Show parents that the directions are displayed in each station. Encourage parents to use the "Talk Together" dialogue as suggestions for how to talk with their children about baptism as they work together on the activity in each station.

Clean Up

(5 minutes)
After twenty or thirty minutes, instruct everyone to help with cleanup. Use "The Cleanup Song" (see page 72) on the **CD** as the signal for cleanup time.

Story Time

(10-15 minutes)
Invite parents and children to sit together for story time. Enjoy the Sing a Verse, Stand 'n Tell Bible Story, Bible Verse Round, and Splash 'n Sing activities during this time.

Visit the Baptismal Font

(10-15 minutes)
Have parents and children go together to the sanctuary to see the baptismal font. Make arrangements for the pastor to tell parents and children about baptism in the church.

Celebration Activities

(15-20 minutes)
You may choose to end the "Parents and Children Learning Together About Baptism" lesson after the visit to the sanctuary, or have parents and children return to the classroom for celebration activities.

Celebration activities include:

Jump!
Share a Snack
Rhyme Time

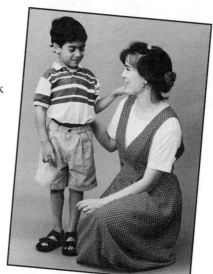

God's Own Dear Son by Daphna Flegal

"**C**ome," the man called to the people. "Come to the water. Come and hear good news."

The man was John the Baptist. He talked to people by the side of the river. He told people the good news about God's Son.
Jesus is God's own dear Son.

"Come into the water," said John. "Tell God you are sorry for the wrong things you have done. Let me baptize you."

Many people came to the river to be baptized by John. Many people heard John tell the good news about God's Son.
Jesus is God's own dear Son.

One day Jesus came to the river. He watched as John baptized people in the water of the Jordan River. He listened as John told people the good news about God's Son.
Jesus is God's own dear Son.

"I want you to baptize me," Jesus said to John. Jesus walked into the water of the Jordan River. John baptized Jesus with the water. John knew that Jesus was God's Son.
Jesus is God's own dear Son.

As Jesus came out of the river, he saw a dove flying in the sky. Jesus heard God's voice. "You are my own dear Son. I am pleased with you." Jesus knew that he was God's Son.
Jesus is God's own dear Son.

(Based on Mark 1:9-11.)

In the River
by Elizabeth Crocker

Down by the *water*,
Jesus found *John*.
In the river,
In the water,
River Jordan, that is.
Baptizing people one by *one*.
In the river,
In the water,
River Jordan, that is.
Jesus said, "John, *baptize me!*"
In the river,
In the water,
River Jordan, that is.
"That's how *God* wants
things to *be."*
In the river,
In the water,
River Jordan, that is.
Jesus was *baptized there* by *John*.
In the river,
In the water,
River Jordan, that is.
God said, "*This* is my
own dear *Son*."
In the river,
In the water,
River Jordan, that is.
The *Spirit* of *God* came
like a *dove*.
In the river,
In the water,
River Jordan, that is.
Jesus knew of *God's* great *love*.
In the river,
In the water,
River Jordan, that is.

Meet 'n Greet

 CD, CD player

- Play "Water Sounds" on the CD as the parents and children arrive.

- Explain the Do-Together Stations to parents.

- **Say: There are several Do-Together Stations around the room for you and your child to enjoy together. The directions are displayed in each station. Suggestions are included for ways you can talk with your child about baptism as you work together in each station. You will have the next twenty to thirty minutes to enjoy the Do-Together Stations with your child. Please stop at the Who's Who Station to make nametags and name bags for you and your child first. You may go to the other stations as you choose. It's not necessary to use all the stations.**

Who's Who Station

 nametags (*page 29*), station directions (*page 28*), crayons, markers, paper punch, scissors, yarn, tape, grocery bags

- Photocopy and cut out the nametags with the water pictures (*page 29*) for each child and each parent.

- Photocopy the directions for the Who's Who Do-Together Station (*page 28*) and display them in the station.

- Set out the crayons, markers, paper punch, scissors, yarn, tape, and grocery bags.

- Explain to parents that they may set their child's name bag on the floor around the edge of the room. As they complete an activity in the Do-Together Stations, they may put their activity (if it is dry) inside their bags.

Storybook Station

 "A Special Child of God" (*page 5*), Bible, quilt or rug, pillows or rocking chair, station directions (*page 30*)

- Photocopy "A Special Child of God" (*page 5*). Set the copy of the story and a Bible on a rug or quilt. Add pillows. Or set a rocking chair or other comfortable chair for parents and children to sit in together.

- Photocopy the directions for the Storytelling Do-Together Station (*page 30*) and display them in the station.

Mix 'n Match Station

 Baptism Today picture cards (*page 19*), scissors, station directions (*page 30*)

- Photocopy and cut apart two sets of the Baptism Today picture cards (*page 19*). Place the cards on the table or on the rug.

- Photocopy the directions for the Mix 'n Match Do-Together Station (*page 30*) and display them in the station.

Touch the Water Station

plastic tablecloth, dishpans, water, smocks, paper cups, sponges, towels, station directions (*page 31*)

- Cover the table or floor with a plastic tablecloth. Place one or two dishpans partially filled with water on the plastic cloth. Add the paper cups and sponges. Have smocks and towels available.

- Photocopy the directions for the Touch the Water Do-Together Station (*page 31*) and display them in the station.

Drip 'n Drop Station

 plastic tablecloth or newspapers, small containers, water, food coloring, paper towels or coffee filters, smocks, station directions (*page 31*)

- Cover the table with a plastic tablecloth or with newspaper.

- Pour a small amount of water into three or four small containers. Place several drops of food coloring in each tub and mix.

- Set out paper towels or coffee filters. Have smocks available.

- Photocopy the directions for the Drip 'n Drop Do-Together Station (**page 31**) and display them in the station.

Dove Derbies Station

 white feathers (available at craft stores), glue, scissors, newspapers, tape, dove derby pattern (*page 33*), station directions (*page 32*)

- Cover the table with newspapers.

- Set out the white feathers and glue.

- Photocopy the dove derby pattern (*page 33*) for each child.

- Photocopy the directions for the Dove Derbies Do-Together Station (*page 32*), and display them in the station.

Doves in Flight Station

 newspapers; paper plates; paper punch, yarn; glitter, shallow trays or box lids, glue or glitter glue; scissors; clothesline or string; clothespins or paper clips; dove pattern (*page 35*), station directions (*page 34*)

- Cover the table with newspapers. Set out the paper plates, paper punch, yarn, and glitter glue or glitter, glue, and two or three shallow trays or box lids.

- Make three or four copies of the dove pattern (*page 35*) and set them on the table.

- Tie a clothesline or string across this station. Have clothespins or paper clips available. Parents will clip the completed dove mobiles to the clothesline or string.

- Photocopy the directions for the Doves in Flight Do-Together Station (*page 34*) and display them in the station.

Water Wash Station

 paintbrushes, newspapers, smocks, plain paper, crayons, blue tempera paint, water, plastic containers, station directions (*page 36*)

- Cover the table with newspapers. Have paint smocks available.

- Set out plain paper and crayons.

- Thin blue tempera paint with water and pour into plastic containers. Set out paintbrushes.

- Photocopy the directions for the Water Wash Do-Together Station (*page 36*) and display them in the station.

Dove Delights Station

shortbread cookie dough, colored sugar or sprinkles, scissors, light cardboard, round cookie cutter, flour, rolling pins, cookie sheets, smocks or aprons, dove pattern (*page 26*), station directions (*page 36*)

• You may want to set this station in the kitchen.

• Prepare shortbread cookie dough according to the recipe below or buy refrigerated sugar cookie dough. Keep the dough refrigerated until ready to use.

• Photocopy and cut out the dove pattern (*page 26*). Trace around the outline onto light cardboard and cut out the center to make a stencil.

• Set out the cookie dough, flour, rolling pins, colored sugar or candy sprinkles, and cookie sheets. Have smocks or aprons available.

• Photocopy the directions for the Dove Delights Do-Together Station (*page 36*) and display them in the station.

• Have parents and children make the cookies according to the directions. Have a teacher (or other volunteer) bake the cookies during the Sing a Verse, Stand 'n Tell Bible Story, Bible Verse Round, and Splash 'n Sing activities.

Shortbread Cookies
1½ cups butter
¾ cups sugar
3 cups flour

Preheat oven to 325 degrees. Cream butter and sugar together. Gradually add flour and mix well. Give each child a golf ball-size piece of dough. Let the child roll the dough into a ball and place it on an ungreased cookie sheet. Help the child place the dove stencil on top of his or her cookie and sprinkle colored sugar or candy sprinkles on top. Remove the stencil. Bake at 325 degrees for fifteen to twenty minutes. Makes twenty-four to thirty cookies.

Clean Up

CD, CD player; towels, *page 72*

• Play "The Cleanup Song" (*page 72*) on the **CD** to signal cleanup time. Have towels available to dry hands and arms.

Sing a Verse

none

• Invite the children to bring their parents and to join you in an open area of the room. Ask two parents to stand facing each other and to hold hands to form a bridge. Have the children and remaining parents stand in a line ready to go through the bridge.

• Sing the song printed below to the tune of "London Bridge." Have the children and parents march under the bridge while you sing. Encourage everyone to sing the song with you.

• When you sing the line, "I am pleased with you," have the parents forming the bridge bring their arms down to catch a child or parent under the bridge. Repeat the song until everyone has been caught.

> God said, "You are my dear son,
>   My dear son, my dear son."
> God said, "You are my dear son.
>   I am pleased with you."

Stand 'n Tell Bible Story

"God's Own Dear Son" (*page 22*), dove derbies

Have the children wear their dove derbies. Invite the children to bring their parents and to join you in your story area.

Say: Our Bible story today is about the time when Jesus was baptized with water in a river. I want you to help me tell the Bible story. Each time I say, "God's Son," I want you to stand up and say, "Jesus is God's own dear Son."

- Let the children practice standing and saying, "Jesus is God's own dear Son."

- Tell the story "God's Own Dear Son" (*page 22*). Emphasize the words *God's Son* each time they appear.

Bible Verse Round

 plastic dove or dove cut from cardboard, CD, CD player, Bible

- Have the children and their parents sit in a circle on the floor. Choose a child to hold the Bible open to Mark 1:11.

- **Say: Jesus saw a dove when he was baptized in the river. When Jesus saw the dove, he heard God's voice. "God said, 'You are my own dear Son. I am pleased with you'" (Mark 1:11, *Good News Bible*, adapted).**

- Have the children and parents repeat the verse with you. Show everyone the dove.

- Play "Water Sounds" from the **CD**. Have the children and parents pass the dove around the circle as the sounds play. Stop the music.

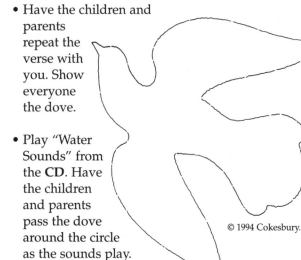

© 1994 Cokesbury.

- Have whoever is holding the dove when you stopped the water sounds stand up. Have the person hold the dove above his or her head.

- Say the Bible verse. Have the person repeat the Bible verse after you.

- Have the person sit down. Continue the game until everyone has been caught holding the dove and has repeated the Bible verse.

Splash 'n Sing

 CD, CD player, *page 38*

- Sing the song "Drip, Drop, Splish, Splash" (*page 38*) on the CD. Encourage the children and parents to sing and move with the song.

Drip, drop,
(*Clap hands.*)
Splish, splash,
(*Pat knees.*)
Trickle, trickle,
(*Wiggle fingers.*)
Flow.
(*Make a sweeping motion with arms.*)

Words and music by James Ritchie. © 1996 James Ritchie.

Visit the Baptismal Font

 name bags

- Invite parents and children to go to the sanctuary to see where people in your church are baptized. Make sure there is water in the baptismal font before taking the visit.

- If you plan to end the lesson at the sanctuary, have parents and children gather their activities and place them in their name bags. Have parents bring their name bags with them to the sanctuary.

- Ask your pastor to meet with you and to speak briefly to the children and their parents about baptism.

- Close with a prayer.

- Or invite parents and children to return to the classroom for Celebration Station activities.

Celebration Station

Use the activities on this page if you choose to have parents and children return to the classroom after the visit to the baptismal font. These activities are designed for fun and fellowship.

Jump!

 blue crepe paper

- Invite the children and their parents to an open area of the room. Tear off three or four long strips of blue crepe paper. Twist the ends of the strips together. Ask two parents to hold the ends of the strips.

- **Say: Jesus was baptized by John in a river. Let's pretend the blue streamers are water in a river.**

- Have the parents holding the strips wiggle the strips back and forth on the floor.

- Have each parent hold his or her child's hand. Let the pairs take turns jumping back and forth over the strips. As each pair jumps, say the following rhyme as you would a jump rope rhyme. (Do not expect the children to jump in time to the rhyme.)

  Wade in the water,
  Wade in the water,
  Wade in the water
  With Jesus and John.

  Jump!
  1, 2, 3, 4,
  And wade in the water
  With Jesus and John.

Share a Snack

 plastic pitcher, cookies, napkins, paper cups, water

- Invite children and parents to sit at the table. Choose children to hand out napkins and paper cups.

- Fill the pitcher with cool water. Pass the pitcher around the table. Encourage parents to let their child pour the water into the cups.

- Give each parent and child a dove cookie made during the Dove Delights Do-Together Station time.

- If you chose not to make cookies during the lesson, ask a volunteer to make the cookies ahead of time.

- **Pray: Thank you, God, for water to drink and to use in baptisms. Thank you for cookies to eat. Amen.**

- Talk about the dove shape on the cookies. Remind the parents and children that when Jesus was baptized, he saw a dove in the sky.

Rhyme Time

 "In the River" rhyme (*page 22*)

- Have the children clean up after sharing the snack. Have everyone sit back down at the table in your story area.

- **Say: Today we have learned about the time when Jesus was baptized. Let's play a rhythm game to remember the story.**

- Use the rhyme "In the River" (*page 22*) with the children and their parents. Say the chorus, "In the river, in the water, River Jordan, that is." Repeat this several times with a steady rhythm. Clap when you say the words *river, water, Jordan,* and *is,* for a total of four claps.

- Practice the chorus several times with the children and parents. Then read the whole rhyme. Encourage the children and parents to clap and say the chorus with you each time. Lead the children and parents in patting their hands on their legs as you say the verses. The syllables printed in italics indicate when you should pat your legs.

- Have parents and children gather their activities and place them inside their name bags to take home.

- Help your child make a nametag and make one nametag for yourself.

- Color the nametags with blue crayons.

- Write the names on the nametags with a marker.

- Use a paper punch to make a hole in the top of the nametag. Measure a length of yarn to easily fit over your child's head. Thread the yarn through the hole and tie the ends of the yarn together to make a nametag necklace. Or tape the nametags to clothing.

- Give your child a paper bag.

- Let your child decorate the bags with crayons or markers.

- Write your child's name on the bag.

- Open the bag and place it along the wall on the floor. Use the bag to store the things you and your child make from each Do-Together Station.

Talk Together

- **Say: The picture on our nametags makes me think about water. Water is very important in our world. Can you think of a way we use water?**

- Talk about the different ways we use water, such as washing dishes, washing clothes, drinking, watering plants, bathing, and cooking.

- **Say: Water is used for something very special in the church. It is used for baptism. Our Bible story today is about the time when Jesus was baptized with water.**

Nametags

29

Storybook Station

- Read the story, "A Special Child of God" with your child. When you finish the story, open the Bible to Mark 1:11.

Talk Together

- **Say: The story of Jesus' baptism is in the Bible.**

- Say the Bible verse, "God said, 'You are my own dear Son. I am pleased with you'" (Mark 1:11, *Good News Bible*, adapted).

Mix 'n Match Station

- Place the baptism picture cards on the table or on the rug. Encourage the children to find the matching pictures.

Talk Together

- **Say: Water is important in our world. We use water to drink, to make things clean, and to help things grow. Water is also important in our church. It is used for baptism. These pictures show some of the ways that our church baptizes people.**

- If your child has been baptized, tell your child about his or her baptism. Talk about when she or he was baptized, who was there to see the baptism, and where the baptism took place.

Touch the Water Station

- Have your child wear a smock to protect her or his clothing. Have towels available to dry hands and arms.

- Encourage your child to pour, dip, and experience the water. Show your child how to dip the sponges into a dishpan of water and then squeeze the excess water out of the sponges.

Talk Together

- Talk about how the water feels. Help your child think about the different ways we use water, such as washing dishes, washing clothes, drinking, watering plants, bathing, and cooking.

- **Say: Water is important in our world. Water is used for drinking and for helping plants grow. Water is used to help make things clean. Water is used for something very special in the church. It is used for baptism.**

Drip 'n Drop Station

- Have your child wear a smock to protect clothing. Give your child a piece of paper towel or a coffee filter.

- Show your child how to dip the edges of the paper towel or coffee filter into the colored water. Help your child notice how the colors blend and change.

Talk Together

- Talk about some of the different ways that we use water (brush teeth, take a bath, swim, wash hands and face, water plants, drink).

- **Say: We use water for so many different things. In the church we use water for something special. We use water for baptism.**

Dove Derbies Station

- Cut out the crown strips for your child.

- Point out the dove on the crown.

- Let your child glue feathers onto the dove.

- Tape or glue one end of the back strip to one end of the dove strip. Measure the strips around your child's head. Tape or glue the remaining strips together to make a crown. Encourage your child to wear the dove derby.

Talk Together

- Remind your child that when Jesus was baptized, he saw a dove in the sky and heard God's voice.

- **Say: Jesus heard God say, "You are my own dear Son. I am pleased with you" (Mark 1:11, *Good News Bible*, adapted).**

- Talk with your child about how people are baptized in your church.

- Explain to your child that when parents or other caregivers bring babies to be baptized, they make a promise. They promise to help children learn about God and God's love as the children grow. The people in the church also make a promise to help the baby grow.

- If your child has been baptized, share your memories of that experience with your child.

- Let your child know that he or she is an important part of your church family. (If your child has not been baptized, let your child know that all children are an important part of the church.)

- Remind your child that God loves each one of us.

TAPE, GLUE OR STAPLE EXTENSIONS...

...SIZE TO EACH HEAD.

Dove Derby Pattern

33

Doves in Flight Station

- Trace the dove pattern onto a paper plate. Cut the dove out for your child. Or let your child cut the dove out using safety scissors.

- Fold the paper plate dove as shown on the dove pattern.

- Let your child brush glue over the paper plate dove.

- Set the dove in a shallow tray or box lid. Shake the glitter over the dove. Shake off excess glitter. Pour the excess glitter back into the glitter container.

- Or let your child decorate the dove with glitter glue.

- Use a paper punch to make a hole in the back of the dove. Thread a piece of yarn through the hole. Tie the ends of the yarn together to make a hanger.

- Use a clothespin or paper clip to hang the dove on the clothesline in this station.

Talk Together

- Remind your child that when Jesus was baptized, he saw a dove in the sky and heard God's voice.

- **Say: Jesus heard God say, "You are my own dear Son. I am pleased with you" (Mark 1:11, *Good News Bible*, adapted).**

- Encourage your child to repeat the Bible verse.

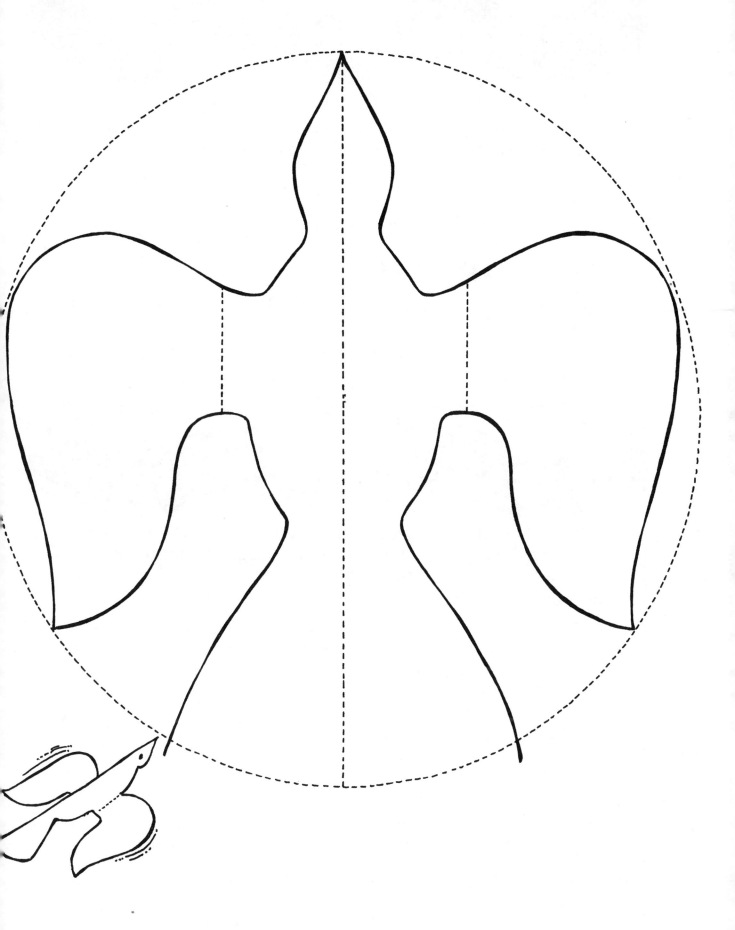

God Is Pleased With Me

Water Wash Station

- Have your child wear a smock to protect his or her clothing.

- Give your child a piece of plain paper. Have your child draw on the paper with crayons. Show your child how to color with heavy marks.

- Show your child how to paint over the crayon drawing with the blue tempera paint. The crayons will show through the paint and will make it look like what your child has drawn is underwater.

Talk Together

- Talk about some of the ways we use water (take a bath, drink, cook, water plants, wash clothes).

- **Say: Water is used for something very special in our church. It is used for baptism.**

Dove Delights Station

- Lightly flour the work surface. Give your child a golf ball-size piece of cookie dough. Let your child roll the dough out flat and use a cookie cutter or plastic cup to cut out a round cookie shape. Place the cookie on the baking sheet.

- Let your child place the dove stencil on top. Show your child how to sprinkle colored sugar or candy sprinkles on top of the cookie shape. Carefully remove the stencil. Point out the picture of the dove left on the cookie.

Talk Together

- Remind your child that when Jesus was baptized, he saw a dove in the sky and heard God's voice.

- **Say: Jesus heard God say, "You are my own dear Son. I am pleased with you" (Mark 1:11, *Good News Bible*, adapted).**

- Encourage your child to repeat the Bible verse.

Parents

You are invited to "Parents and Children Learning Together About Baptism"

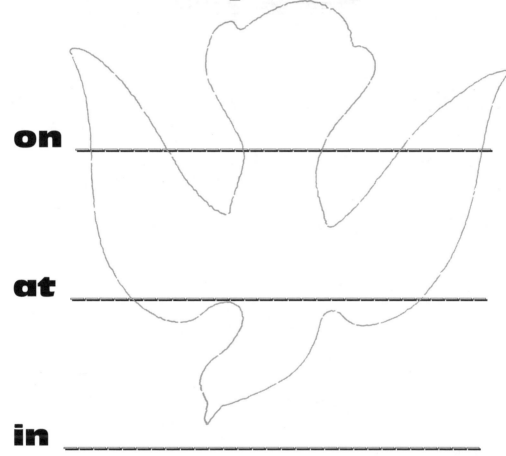

on _____

at _____

in _____

Enjoy "Do-Together" Stations that will help you talk with your child about the sacrament of baptism.

Drip, Drip, Splish, Splash

Drip, drop, splish, splash,

trick - le, trick - le, flow;

wa - ter, wa - ter, ev - ery - where,
love is with me ev - ery - where,
God is with me ev - ery - where,
wa - ter and the love of God,

ev - ery-where I go.

WORDS and MUSIC: James Ritchie
© 1996 James Ritchie

Scriptures For Communion

Matthew 26:17-20, 26-27; Mark 14:12-17, 22-24; Luke 22:7-20

Understanding the Bible Verses

The story of Jesus' last meal with the disciples is in the Gospels of Matthew, Mark, and Luke. In Luke, Jesus breaks bread and says, "Do this in memory of me" (Luke 22:19, *Good News Bible*).

Jesus and his disciples ate the meal together in celebration of the Passover. The Passover meal reminded the Hebrews of the Israelites' escape from slavery in Egypt. The disciples had celebrated Passover all their lives, and it would have been expected for them to celebrate it in the company of Jesus this particular year.

Jesus gave the elements of the Passover meal the new interpretation that became the foundation of the Christian church's celebration of the Lord's Supper, the Eucharist, also known as Holy Communion.

Our symbols for Communion, the bread and the cup, were ordinary elements of the meal Jesus and the disciples shared. But because of Jesus' new interpretation of those items during the meal, they have become sacred symbols — reminders of Jesus' body and blood, given for us.

Understanding Your Children

Young children have difficulty understanding abstract concepts and symbolism such as the bread and the cup symbolizing the body and blood of Jesus. They may be confused, and even frightened, by Jesus' talking about giving up his body and blood.

Instead of focusing on the symbolism, find ways to relate Holy Communion to experiences in your children's lives. Your children can relate to sharing a meal with special friends, or remembering friends through special events.

Young children can understand that Communion is a time when we remember Jesus. Give your children

tangible experiences to help that understanding. Take your children to visit the sanctuary where Communion is observed. Show the children the Communion table. Let the children kneel at the Communion rail and see the place where empty cups are left. Let them touch the plate and cup. Invite them to drink juice and eat bread. Help children use their eyes, ears, touch, and taste to begin to understand the sacrament that helps us remember Jesus.

Talk to your pastor and your parents if you want to serve Communion as part of these lessons on Communion.

Developing Your Faith

Read Luke 22:7-20. Jesus told his disciples to remember him through the breaking of the bread and the drinking from the cup. When you think of Jesus, what is the first thing you remember? Do you remember the stories of his birth? Do you remember the stories of his death and his resurrection? Say a prayer thanking God for the gift of Jesus.

Read Mark 14:12-16. Jesus and his disciples observed the Passover meal together in the upper room of a house. This meal became the foundation

for our sacrament of Communion. Think for a moment about your own Communion experiences. What makes some memories stand out more than others? Was it the place or the people with whom you shared the sacrament?

Read Matthew 26:17-20, 26-27. We have a new relationship with God through Jesus' sacrifice. What does this new relationship mean to you? Give thanks for Jesus and his great gift to you and all people.

Communion

Do this in memory of me.
(Luke 22:19, *Good News Bible*)

Lesson Overview

✓ Learning Experiences	✓ Supplies	✓ Before Class
Who's Who	CD, CD player, nametags (*page 65*), crayons or markers, paper punch, scissors, yarn or tape	Photocopy and cut out nametags.
Bake Bread	flour, baking sheets, canned or frozen bread dough (thaw first) or ingredients for Communion bread, smocks or aprons	
Clean Up	CD, CD player, damp dishcloths, *page 72*	
Remember 'n Sing	none	
Touch 'n Tell Bible Story	"A Special Meal With Friends" story (*page 41*), plastic grapes (available at craft stores), paper cup, white felt	
Bible Verse Find	plastic grapes, Bible	
Sing a Round	CD, CD player, plastic grapes	
Memory Mosaics	colored tissue paper, bread and cup pictures (*page 46*), glue, scissors, pencils, large piece of paper, marker	Photocopy bread and cup pictures.
Clean Up	CD, CD player, *page 72*	
Memory Mayhem	plastic grapes, four Communion cups, one paper cup, white felt, plastic pitcher	
Taste the Bread	napkins, bread made earlier in lesson, butter, honey, plastic knife or spoon	
Time to Go	memory mosaics, parent's page (*page 45*)	Photocopy the parent's page.

A Special Meal With Friends

by Susan Isbell

"**S**upper is ready," Jesus said. "It's time to eat."

Jesus' friends came to the table.

"Thank you, God, for this food," Jesus said.

His friends were ready to eat.

"The food is good," said Jesus. "Eat it and remember that I love you."

His friends were hungry. They ate the bread and meat that Jesus gave them.

"The drink is cold," said Jesus. "Drink it and remember that I love you."

Jesus' friends were thirsty. They drank all that was in the cup.

"You are my best friends," Jesus said. "Each time you eat together, remember that I am your friend."

His friends told Jesus that they would remember.

"You are my best friends," Jesus said. "Each time you eat together, remember that I love you."

His friends told Jesus that they would remember.

(Based on Luke 22:7-20)

Copyright © 1994, 1997 Cokesbury

Who's Who

CD, CD player, nametags (*page 65*), crayons or markers, paper punch, scissors, yarn or tape

• Play "Communion Songs" from the **CD** as the children arrive. Greet each child by name. If you do not know the children's names, make nametags.

• Photocopy and cut out nametags (*page 65*). Let each child color a nametag. Write the child's name on the nametag. Punch a hole in the top of the nametag. Measure yarn to fit over the child's head. Thread the yarn through the hole; tie the ends to make a necklace. Or tape the nametag to the child's clothing.

• **Say: Our nametags show a loaf of bread and a cup. The pictures make me think about a special meal Jesus ate with his friends. Jesus shared bread and juice at the special meal. When Jesus shared bread and juice, he asked his friends to remember him.**

• Talk about Jesus. Help the children remember Jesus' birth, Jesus and the children, and Jesus' baptism.

Bake Bread

flour, baking sheets, canned or frozen bread dough (thaw first) or ingredients for Communion bread, smocks or aprons, baking sheets

• Choose an activity below to help the children experience baking bread. Consider having the children make enough loaves so that the bread may be used for Communion with your congregation. Tell the children they will eat the bread later in the lesson.

Bake Bread

• Have the children wear smocks or aprons and wash their hands. Lightly flour the table in front of each child. Give each child a section of canned or frozen bread dough. Let the children knead the dough and shape it however they wish. Place the shapes on a baking sheet. Have each child make two, one to eat in class and one to take home or use in Communion. Bake according to the recipe.

Bake Communion Bread

• Have the children wear smocks or aprons and wash their hands. Let the children take turns adding and mixing the ingredients. Lightly flour the table in front of each child. Give each child a section of

dough. Let the children knead the dough and shape the dough into flat loaves. Place the loaves on a baking sheet. Bake according to the recipe.

Talk About the Experiences

• **Say: Jesus ate a special meal with his friends. Our bread can help us remember that special meal.**

Clean Up

CD, CD player, damp dishcloths, *page 72*

• Play "The Cleanup Song" (*page 72*) from the **CD**. Encourage all the children to help clean up. Have damp dishcloths on hand to clean up flour.

Remember 'n Sing

• **Say: Jesus ate a special meal with his friends. Jesus shared bread and juice at the special meal. When Jesus shared the bread and juice, he asked his friends to remember him. Let's remember Jesus.**

• Have the children hold hands and stand in a circle. Sing the following words to the tune of "The Farmer in the Dell." Have the children walk in a circle as you sing.

Communion Bread

¾ cup butter
¾ cup sugar
¼ teaspoon salt
1 cup sour milk or add 1 tablespoon vinegar to
   1 cup milk
¼ teaspoon baking soda
1 teaspoon baking powder
4 cups all-purpose flour

Preheat oven to 350 degrees. Cream butter and sugar. Add remaining ingredients in the order listed. Mix well. Give each child a golf ball-size piece of dough to shape into a flat loaf. Place each loaf on a baking sheet for ten to fifteen minutes. Cool before eating. Makes 24 to 28 small loaves.

Oh, we remember Jesus.
Oh, we remember Jesus.
Jesus shared a special meal.
Oh, we remember Jesus.

• Stop walking; say: **I remember Jesus is God's son.**

Sing the next stanza. Have the children drop their hands and do the motions.

Oh, Jesus is God's son. (*Put hands over heart.*)
Oh, Jesus is God's son. (*Put hands over heart.*)
We remember our friend Jesus. (*Turn around.*)
Oh, Jesus is God's son. (*Put hands over heart.*)

• Sing the first stanza of the song again. Have the children hold hands and walk around the circle. Stop walking.

• Say: **I remember Jesus loved the children.**

• On the next stanza, have the children drop hands and do the suggested motions.

Oh, Jesus loved the children. (*Hug self.*)
Oh, Jesus loved the children. (*Hug self.*)
We remember our friend Jesus. (*Turn around.*)
Oh, Jesus loved the children. (*Hug self.*)

• Sing the first stanza of the song a third time. Have the children hold hands and walk around the circle.

Touch 'n Tell Bible Story

"A Special Meal With Friends" story (*page 41*), plastic grapes (available at craft stores), paper cup, white felt

• Spread white felt where the children can see it. Place a cup and the grapes on the felt.

• Say: **Our Bible story today is about the time when Jesus shared a special meal with his friends.**

• Use the story "A Special Meal With Friends" (*page 41*) to tell the children the story of the Last Supper.

• Say: **Jesus shared bread and juice with his friends at the special meal. When Jesus shared the bread and juice, he asked his friends to remember him. We have a special meal in church to remember Jesus. We call the special meal Communion.**

• Have the children come up one at a time to touch the grapes and cup.

• Say: **(Child's name) can remember Jesus.**

Bible Verse Find

plastic grapes, Bible

• Have the children sit on the floor. Choose a child to hold the Bible open to Luke 22:19.

• Say: **Jesus shared bread and juice with his friends at a special meal. Jesus asked his friends to remember him. Jesus said, "Do this in memory of me" (Luke 22:19, *Good News Bible*).**

• Show the children the plastic grapes.

• Say: **The juice Jesus shared at the meal came from grapes. Grapes help us remember the special meal.**

• Choose a child to cover his or her eyes. Hide the grapes. Have the child uncover her or his eyes and search for the grapes. When the child is close to the grapes, have the other children clap. When the child moves away, have the children sit quietly.

• When the child finds the grapes, have the child bring the grapes and stand in front of the other children. Say the Bible verse for the child. Have the child repeat the Bible verse after you. Have the child sit down. Continue until every child has had a turn.

Sing-a-Round

CD, CD player, plastic grapes

• Have the children sit in a circle. Sing "A Special Meal" from the **CD**. On "He passed around the juice and bread," pass the plastic grapes around the circle.

A Special Meal
Jesus shared a special meal,
Special meal, special meal.
Jesus shared a special meal
So many years ago.

He passed around the juice and bread,
Juice and bread, juice and bread.
He passed around the juice and bread
So many years ago.

We can share this special meal,
Special meal, special meal.
We can share this special meal
With friends we've come to know.
Words: Tim Edmonds; © 1996 Cokesbury.

Memory Mosaics

 colored tissue paper, bread and cup pictures (*page 46*), glue, scissors, pencils. large piece of paper, marker

- Photocopy the bread and cup picture (*page 46*) for each child. Cut colored tissue paper into one-inch squares. Give each child a picture. Let the children make mosaics by gluing on tissue paper squares. Have older children wrap tissue paper squares around the eraser end of pencils. Place a dot of glue on the bottom of the squares while still wrapped. Use pencils to press the squares onto the pictures to give them a three-dimensional look.

- **Say: Jesus shared bread and juice with his friends at a special meal. When Jesus shared the bread and juice, he asked his friends to remember him.**

- Read the Bible verse printed on the pictures to the children. Have the children repeat the verse.

- **Say: We have a special meal in church to remember Jesus. We call the special meal Communion. We eat bread and drink juice at Communion.**

- Display the children's pictures on a bulletin board or wall. Make a sign that says "A Special Meal."

Clean Up

 CD, CD player, *page 72*

- Play "The Cleanup Song" (*page 72*) from the **CD**. Encourage all the children to help clean up. Plan activities that are easy to clean up at the close of the lesson to keep children busy while they wait for parents. If children are active, they will be less likely to become anxious if other parents arrive first.

Memory Mayhem

 plastic grapes, four Communion cups, one paper cup, white felt, plastic pitcher

- Spread the white felt out on a rug or table. Place the plastic grapes, three or four Communion cups, a paper cup, and a small pitcher on the felt.

- Say: Jesus had a special meal with his friends. At the special meal he shared bread and juice. The grapes (*show the grapes*) **can help us remember the special meal. We have a special meal in church to remember Jesus. We call the special meal Communion. Sometimes we use small Communion cups (*show the Communion cups*) like these when we have Communion. Sometimes we use a pitcher (*show the pitcher*) to pour the juice into a cup (*show the cup*).**

- Have the children cover their eyes. Remove one item from the felt and hide it behind your back. Have the children open their eyes. Let the children remember what item is missing. When the children have named the item, show the children the item hidden behind your back. Repeat the game and remove a different item each time.

Taste the Bread

 napkins, bread made earlier in lesson, butter, honey, plastic knife or spoon

- Choose children to hand out napkins. Serve the bread made earlier in the lesson. Let the children add butter and honey.

- **Note: Be careful of children with food allergies.**

- **Say: Jesus shared a special meal with his friends. They ate bread at that special meal. We have a special meal at our church to remember Jesus. It is called Communion. We eat bread at Communion.**

- **Pray: Thank you, God, for Jesus. Thank you for bread. Amen.**

Time to Go

 memory mosaics, parent's page (*page 45*)

- Give the children their memory mosaics to take home. Give parents a parent's page (*page 45*). Tell parents about any additional lessons you have planned as part of this study.

- Encourage parents to take their children to worship when Communion will take place.

Parent's Page

Communion is an important sacrament in the church.

Communion, or the Lord's Supper, is one way we remember Jesus' great love for each one of us. It is a sign of Christ's sacrifice for us. Communion also reminds us of the love that Christians share with one another. Communion is a gift of grace freely offered to all persons, including children. Today's lesson on Communion introduced your child to the sacrament and to the Bible story about the Last Supper. This Bible story was explained in terms of the meal, the love of friends, and the memories that were made, instead of in the abstract terms of the symbolism of the body and blood of Christ.

Look at the Bible

Open your family's Bible to Luke 22:7-20. Show the page to your child.

Say: The Bible tells us the story about the time when Jesus shared a special meal with his friends. At the special meal Jesus asked his friends to remember him.

Read the Bible verse, "Do this in memory of me" (Luke 22:19, *Good News Bible*).

Talk with your child about things that she or he remembers about Jesus.

Taste the Bread

Enjoy making cinnamon bread with your child.

Easy Cinnamon Bread

1 can refrigerated crescent dinner rolls
ground cinnamon
sugar
softened butter

Heat the oven to 375 degrees. Unroll the dough to form eight triangles. Place the triangles on an ungreased baking sheet. Spread softened butter on each triangle. Sprinkle the cinnamon and sugar over the butter. Roll each triangle into a crescent shape. Bake ten to twelve minutes or until golden brown.

Sing!

Sing together the song "A Special Meal" to the tune of "Mary Had a Little Lamb."

A Special Meal
Jesus shared a special meal,
Special meal, special meal.
Jesus shared a special meal
So many years ago.

He passed around the juice and bread,
Juice and bread, juice and bread.
He passed around the juice and bread
So many years ago.

We can share this special meal,
Special meal, special meal.
We can share this special meal
With friends we've come to know.

Words: Tim Edmonds.
© 1996 Cokesbury.

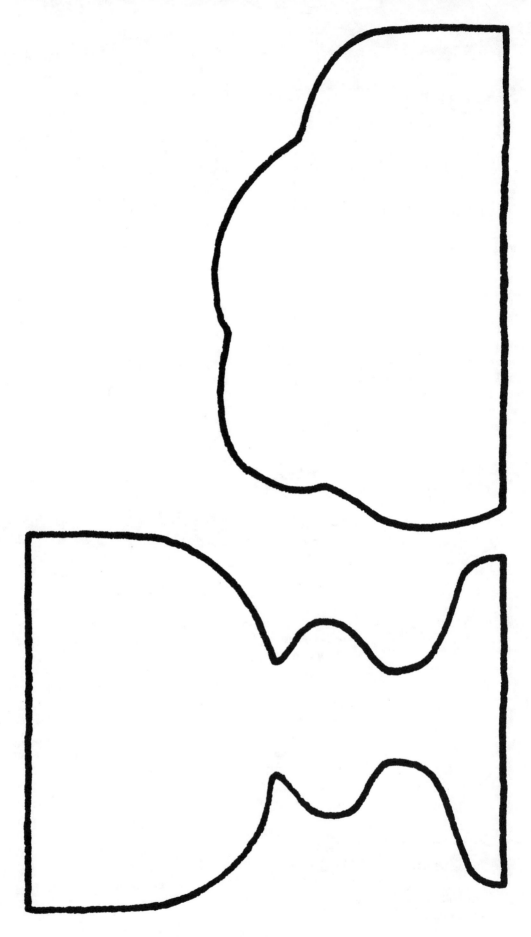

Bread and Cup

Communion

Do this in memory of me.
(Luke 22:19, *Good News Bible*)

Lesson Overview

✓ Learning Experiences	✓ Supplies	✓ Before Class
Who's Who	CD, CD player, nametags (*page 65*), crayons, marker, paper punch, scissors, yarn or tape	Photocopy and cut out nametags.
Touch the Water	construction paper, scissors, crayons or markers, tape; or lunch-size paper bags, strips of construction paper, glue	
Touch 'n Tell	Communion cups, plastic pitcher, plastic grapes (available at craft stores), one paper cup, white felt, bread basket	
Clean Up	CD, CD player, *page 72*	
Finger Frolics	none	
Move 'n Tell Bible Story	"Remember Me" story (*page 48*)	
Bible Verse Find	plastic grapes, Bible	
Sing-a-Round	CD, CD player, plastic grapes	
Communion Books	Communion book pages (*pages 54 and 55*), crayons, masking tape; scissors; construction paper; stapler, staples, or paper punch, yarn	Photocopy Communion book pages for each child.
Clean Up	CD, CD player, *page 72*	
Visit the Sanctuary	Communion items	
Taste the Bread	napkins, different kinds of bread, bread baskets	
Memory Hop	optional: masking tape or chalk	
Time to Go	Communion books, parent's page (*page 53*) (optional: *page 71*)	Photocopy parent's page.

Remember Me by Joyce Riffe

"**W**here will we eat tonight?" asked Jesus' friends. (*Raise hands and shrug shoulders.*) It was time to get ready for the special meal that Jesus and his friends were going to eat together.

"Go into the city," said Jesus. (*Point finger to indicate place far away.*) "Look for a man carrying a jar of water. Follow him to a house. Ask the owner of the house to show you a room where we can have our special meal."

The friends went into the city. (*Walk in place.*) They found a man carrying a jar of water. They followed him to a house, where the owner showed them a large room upstairs. They worked together to get ready for the special meal.

Jesus and his friends climbed up the steps to the room. (*Pretend to climb stairs.*) They sat down around the table. They ate the food and talked with one another.

While they were eating, Jesus held up a loaf of bread. (*Raise hands as if holding a loaf of bread.*) "Thank you, God, for this bread," said Jesus. Then he broke the bread into smaller pieces. Jesus gave a piece of bread to each of his friends. "When you eat this," said Jesus, "remember me. Remember what good friends we have been. Remember all the things we have done together."

Jesus picked up a cup. (*Raise hands as if holding a cup.*) "Thank you, God, for things to drink." Then he passed the cup to each of his friends. "Drink this," he said, "and remember me. Remember all about my life. Remember all the things I have taught you. Remember that God loves you." (*Cross hands over heart.*)

(*Based on Mark 14:12-16, 22-25.*)

© 1995 Cokesbury.

© 1994 Cokesbury.

48

Who's Who

CD, CD player, nametags (*page 65*), crayons, marker, paper punch, scissors, yarn or tape

- Play "Communion Songs" on the **CD** as the children arrive. Greet each child by name. If you do not know the children's names, use nametags (*page 65*) again this week. Have nametags (*page 42*) available for children who were not present for the first lesson.

- As you give each child his or her other nametag, **say: The picture on our nametags shows a loaf of bread and a cup. The picture makes me think about a special meal that Jesus ate with his friends. Jesus shared bread and juice with his friends at the special meal. When Jesus shared the bread and juice, he asked his friends to remember him.**

- Talk with the children about what they remember about Jesus. Help the children remember the stories of Jesus' birth, the story of Jesus and the children, and the story of Jesus' baptism.

Touch the Water

construction paper, scissors, crayons or markers, tape; or lunch-size paper bags, strips of construction paper, glue

- Use construction paper to make bread baskets. Give each child a piece of construction paper. Write each child's name on the paper. Let the children decorate the paper with crayons or markers.

- Clip the corners of each paper in about 2½ inches. Turn the baskets so that the plain side faces up. Help the children fold up and overlap each corner. Tape each corner together.

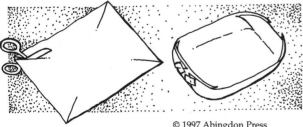

© 1997 Abingdon Press

- **Say: We remember that Jesus ate a special meal with his friends. Our church has a special meal to remember Jesus. It is called Communion. At Communion we eat bread and drink juice and remember Jesus.**

- Or let the children make baskets out of lunch-size paper bags. If you have younger children, do steps 1 and 2 before class. Let the children glue on strips of construction paper instead of weaving.

- Open the bags.

- Fold the top edge of the bag to the inside until it touches the bottom of the bag. Fold in half again.

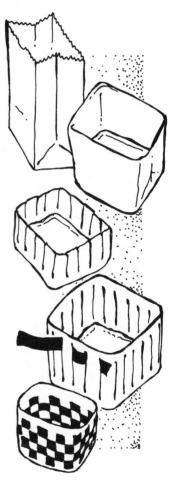

- Make cuts through the fold about one inch apart. Leave approximately one inch around the base of the sack uncut. Unfold the second fold.

- Let each child choose two or three strips of construction paper. Show the children how to weave the strip over and under each cut in the bag.

- Tape the ends together when you have made one complete round. Begin another strip.

- Save the baskets to use later in the lesson.

Ages 3–5, Teacher

49

Touch 'n Tell

 Communion cups, plastic pitcher, plastic grapes (available at craft stores), one paper cup, white felt, bread basket

- Display the Communion cups, the plastic pitcher, one paper cup, the white felt, plastic grapes, and one bread basket on a table.

- Have the children sit on the floor.

- Say the following rhyme. Choose one child to name in the rhyme. Have the child stand up and listen to the clue you give about one of the items on the table. Then have the child go to the table and touch whatever is named in the rhyme. After the child touches the item, talk about how the item is used in Communion. Repeat the game until every child has a turn.

Touch and tell,
Touch and tell.
(*Child's name*), stand up
And listen well.
Then go to the table to
Touch and tell . . .

- . . . something round and purple, that comes in a bunch. (*grapes*)
- . . . something small and clear, that you drink from. (*Communion cups*)
- . . . something white and soft, that's used to cover things up. (*white felt to represent cloth covers*)
- . . . something that's used to hold bread. (*bread basket*)
- . . . something used to pour grape juice into cups. (*pitcher*)
- . . . something (*name color of paper cup*) that can be used to hold grape juice. (*cup*)

Clean Up

 CD, CD player, *page 72*

- Play "The Cleanup Song" (*page 72*) from the **CD** to signal cleanup time. Encourage all the children to participate.

Finger Frolics

 none

- Have the children join you in your story area.

- Say: The Bible story tells about a special meal Jesus ate with his friends. Jesus wanted his friends to remember him. What do you remember about Jesus?

- Encourage the children to tell you what they remember about Jesus.

- Use the following fingerplay with the children.

Five happy children came to church one day.
They remembered Jesus in a very special way.
(*Wiggle all five fingers.*)
The first child remembered
That Jesus is God's son.
(*Hold up one finger.*)
The second child remembered
He loves me and everyone.
(*Hold up two fingers.*)
The third child remembered
How Jesus shared some bread.
(*Hold up three fingers.*)
The fourth child remembered
"Drink from this cup," he said.
(*Hold up four fingers.*)
The fifth child remembered
The special meal he led.
(*Hold up five fingers.*)
Five happy children came to church one day.
They remembered Jesus in a very special way.
(*Wiggle all five fingers.*)

Move 'n Tell Bible Story

 "Remember Me" story (*page 48*)

- Say: Our Bible story today is about the time when Jesus shared a special meal with his friends.

- Tell the story "Remember Me" (*page 48*). Encourage the children to do the motions with you.

Bible Verse Find

plastic grapes, Bible

- Have the children sit on the floor. Choose a child to hold the Bible open to Luke 22:19.

- Say: Jesus shared bread and juice with his friends at a special meal. When Jesus shared the bread and juice, he asked his friends to remember him. Jesus said, "Do this in memory of me" (Luke 22:19, *Good News Bible*).

- Have the children repeat the verse with you. Show the children the plastic grapes.

- Say: The juice Jesus shared at the special meal came from grapes. Grapes can help us remember the special meal.

- Choose one child to be "it." Have the child put a hand over his or her eyes. Hide the grapes somewhere in your room.

- Have the child uncover her or his eyes. Let the child search the room to find the grapes. When the child is close to the grapes, have the other children clap their hands. When the child moves away from the grapes, have the other children fold their hands in their laps.

- When the child finds the grapes, have the child bring the grapes and stand in front of the other children. Say the Bible verse for the child. Have the child repeat the Bible verse after you.

- Have the child sit down. Continue the game until every child has had an opportunity to find the grapes and repeat the Bible verse.

Sing-a-Round

CD, plastic grapes, CD player

- Have the children sit in a circle. Sing together the song "A Special Meal" from the CD. The tune is "Mary Had a Little Lamb."

- On the phrase, "He passed around the juice and bread," start passing the plastic grapes around the circle.

A Special Meal
Jesus shared a special meal,
Special meal, special meal.
Jesus shared a special meal
So many years ago.

He passed around the juice and bread,
Juice and bread, juice and bread.
He passed around the juice and bread
So many years ago.

We can share this special meal,
Special meal, special meal.
We can share this special meal
With friends we've come to know.

Words: Tim Edmonds.
© 1996 Cokesbury.

Communion Books

Communion book pages (*pages 54 and 55*), crayons, masking tape; scissors; construction paper; stapler, staples or paper punch, yarn

- Photocopy the Communion book pages (*pages 54 and 55*) for each child. Cut apart the pages.

- Let each child decorate the pages with crayons.

- Give each child a piece of construction paper. Have each child choose three different colors of crayons. Use masking tape to tape the three crayons together. Let the children decorate the papers by coloring with the crayon trios.

© 1995 Cokesbury

- Show the children how to fold the construction paper in half to make a cover for their Communion books. Help each child stack his or her Communion book pages in order and place them inside the cover. Staple the left-hand side of the books to secure the pages. Or use a paper punch to make holes along the left-hand side. Tie yarn through the holes.

Clean Up

CD, CD player, *page 72*

- Play "The Cleanup Song" (*page 72*) from the **CD** to signal cleanup time once again. Have the children help put away crayons and glue.

Visit the Sanctuary

Communion items

- Take the children to the sanctuary to see where people in your church celebrate Communion. Ask your pastor or Communion steward to set out the items your church uses for Communion.

- **Say: Our church has a special meal to remember Jesus. It is called Communion. At Communion we eat bread and drink juice and remember Jesus.**

- Ask your pastor to meet you and briefly speak to the children about Communion.

- Let the children kneel at the altar rail if that is how your church serves Communion.

Taste the Bread

napkins, different kinds of bread, bread baskets

- Plan easy-to-cleanup activities at the close of the lesson to keep the children involved while they wait for parents to arrive.

- Place different kinds of breads in the bread baskets made by the children (see page 49). Choose breads that represent different cultures, such as pita bread, Hawaiian bread, and German rye bread.

- Choose children to hand out napkins. Let the children taste the breads. Remind the children that the church has a special meal called Communion when we eat bread and drink juice and remember Jesus. Christians all over the world celebrate Communion.

- **Pray: Thank you, God, for bread. Amen.**

Memory Hop

optional: masking tape or chalk

- Use masking tape or chalk to make a hopscotch pattern on the floor similar to the one below.

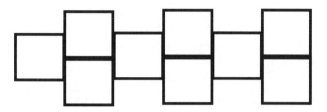

- Have the children hop on one foot on each single square and on two feet on each double square.

- As the children hop, have the children say the Bible verse from Luke 22:19.

> "Do
> (*Hop on one foot.*)
> this
> (*Hop on two feet.*)
> in
> (*Hop on one foot.*)
> memory
> (*Hop on two feet.*)
> of
> (*Hop on one foot.*)
> me."
> (*Hop on two feet.*)

- If you choose not to make a hopscotch pattern on the floor, have the children move in place using the same hopping pattern.

Time to Go

Communion books, parent's page (*page 53*) **(optional:** *page 71*)

- Give the children their Communion books.

- Photocopy the parent's page (*page 53*) for each family. If you are offering the "Children and Parents Learning Together About Communion" lesson, photocopy the note on page 71 to give to parents.

- Encourage parents to take their children to worship when Communion will take place.

Parent's Page

Today your child learned about the special meal Jesus shared with his disciples. Jesus asked his friends to remember him when they ate the bread and drank the juice. The church has a special meal where we eat bread and drink juice and remember Jesus. This meal is called Communion.

Look at the Bible

Make plans to take your child to worship the next time your church is celebrating Communion. The Communion table in The United Methodist Church is an open table. This means that all persons, including children, are invited to share the bread and juice and remember Jesus.

Open your family's Bible to Luke 22:7-20. Show the page to your child.

Say: The Bible tells us about the time when Jesus shared a special meal with his friends. At the special meal Jesus asked his friends to remember him.

Read the Bible verse, "Do this in memory of me" (Luke 22:19, *Good News Bible*).

Talk with your child about things he or she remembers about Jesus.

Taste the Bread

Jesus and his friends shared bread at their meal together. Enjoy making corn muffins with your child. Use the recipe printed below for mixing fun.

> ### Muffin Mixers
>
> corn muffin mix
> ingredients needed for mix
> large resealable plastic bag
> muffin or cupcake papers
> muffin pan
> spoon
>
> Use a resealable plastic bag instead of a mixing bowl. Add the ingredients as indicated on the corn muffin mix in the bag. Securely seal the bag. Let the child squish and shake the bag to mix the ingredients. Line a muffin pan with muffin or cupcake papers. Spoon the batter into the muffin pan. Bake according to the directions.

Memory Hop

Do the memory hop with your child. Hop on one foot and then on two feet as indicated below. As you hop, say the Bible verse from Luke 22:19.

"Do
(Hop on one foot.)
this
(Hop on two feet.)
in
(Hop on one foot.)
memory
(Hop on two feet.)
of
(Hop on one foot.)
me."
(Hop on two feet.)

Parent's Page

They ate and drank together.

Jesus had a special meal with friends.

Communion Book

From *Touch the Water, Taste the Bread, Ages 3–5*. © 1998 Cokesbury. Art © 1995 Cokesbury. Reprinted by permission.

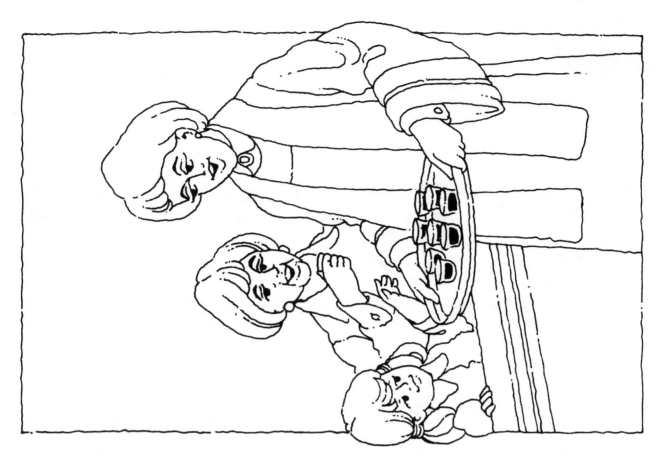

called Holy Communion.

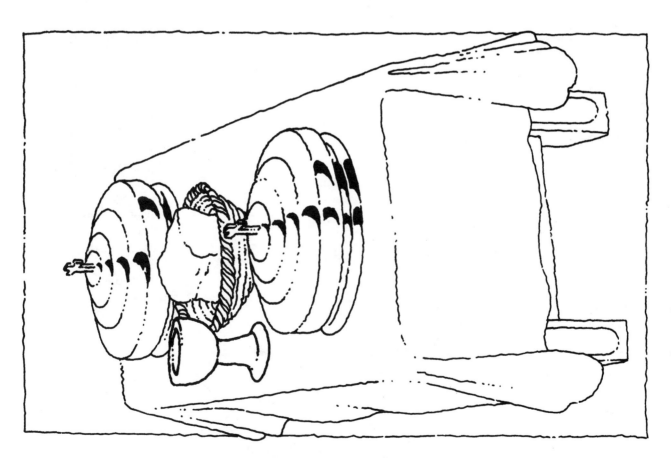

In church we have a special meal

Communion Book

Communion

Do this in memory of me.
(Luke 22:19, *Good News Bible*)

Lesson Overview

✓ Learning Experiences	✓ Supplies	✓ Before Class
Meet 'n Greet	CD, CD player	
Who's Who Station	see page 59	Photocopy and cut out nametags. Photocopy and display directions.
Storybook Station	see page 59	Photocopy and display station directions.
Mix 'n Match Station	see page 59	Photocopy and display station directions.
Discovery Station	see page 59	Photocopy and display station directions.
Place Mat Station	see page 60	Photocopy and display station directions.
Supper Scene Station	see page 60	Photocopy supper scene. Photocopy and display station directions.
Purple Prints Station	see page 60	Photocopy and display station directions.
Bread Station	see page 60	Photocopy and display station directions.
Clean Up	CD, CD player, page 72	
Remember 'n Sing	none	
Sign 'n Tell Bible Story	"We Remember Jesus" story (page 58)	
Bible Verse Find	plastic grapes, Bible	
Sing-a-Round	CD, CD player, plastic grapes	
Celebrate Communion	name bags	
Celebration Station	see page 63	

Touch the Water, Taste the Bread

Parents and Children Learning Together About Communion

The lesson "Parents and Children Learning Together About Communion" is designed for parents and young children to interact with one another. This will provide opportunities for parents and children to explore and experience together these important sacraments in ways that are appealing and meaningful to young children. Use the lesson as part of a three-lesson series on Communion, as part of a six-lesson series on the sacraments, or as a stand-alone lesson on Communion.

Suggested Schedule: (45 minutes to 1½ hours)

Do-Together Stations

(20-30 minutes)
Set up several Do-Together Stations for parents and children to explore. Choose the number of stations based on your room space and the number of people you will have present. If your classroom does not seem big enough, consider moving this lesson to your fellowship hall. Or move quiet activities into a hallway. You may also want to use the kitchen for activities involving food preparation.

Photocopy the directions (pages 64-70) for each station and display the directions in the station.

Explain to parents that they are to stay with their children and to explore the Do-Together Stations for the next twenty to thirty minutes. Show parents that the directions are displayed in each station. Encourage parents to use the "Talk Together" dialogue as suggestions on how to talk with their children about Communion as they work together on the activity in each station.

Clean Up

(5 minutes)
After twenty or thirty minutes, instruct everyone to help with cleanup. Use "The Cleanup Song" (see page 72) on the **CD** as the signal for cleanup time.

Story Time

(10-15 minutes)
Invite parents and children to sit together for story time. Enjoy the Remember 'n Sing, Sign 'n Tell Bible Story, Bible Verse Find, and Sing-a-Round activities during this time.

Celebrate Communion

(10-15 minutes)
Have parents and children go together to the sanctuary to see where your congregation celebrates Communion. Make arrangements for the pastor to tell parents and children about Communion. You also may want to make arrangements for the pastor to serve Communion to the parents and their children.

Celebration Activities

(15-30 minutes)
You may choose to end the "Parents and Children Learning Together About Communion" lesson after the visit to the sanctuary, or have parents and children return to the classroom for celebration activities.

Celebration activities include:
Feast
  Together
Memory
  Circle
Guess Who?

We Remember Jesus

by Sharilyn S. Adair and Daphna Flegal

We remember that Jesus was the baby born at Christmas.

We remember Jesus.

We remember that Jesus loved the little children.

We remember Jesus.

We remember that Jesus is God's son.

We remember Jesus.

We remember that Jesus taught us that God loves each one of us.

We remember Jesus.

We remember that Jesus shared a special meal with his friends.

We remember Jesus.

We remember that at the special meal, Jesus held up a loaf of bread. He thanked God for things to eat. Then Jesus broke the bread into little pieces. He gave a piece of bread to each of his friends.

We remember Jesus.

© 1996 Cokesbury

We remember that at the special meal, Jesus held up a cup. He thanked God for things to drink. Then Jesus passed the cup to each of his friends.

We remember Jesus.

We remember Jesus whenever we drink juice and eat bread together at a special meal called Communion.

We remember Jesus.

We remember that Jesus said, "Do this in memory of me."

We remember Jesus.

We remember the cross and Jesus' great love for us.

We remember Jesus.

Meet 'n Greet

CD, CD player

- Play "Communion Songs" on the CD as the parents and children arrive.

- Explain the Do-Together Stations to parents.

- **Say: There are several Do-Together Stations around the room for you and your child to enjoy together. The directions are displayed in each station. Suggestions are on the directions for ways you can talk with your child about Communion as you work together on the activity in each station. You will have the next twenty to thirty minutes to enjoy the Do-Together Stations with your child. Please stop at the Who's Who Station to make nametags and name bags for you and your child first. You may go to the other stations as you choose. It's not necessary to use all the stations.**

Who's Who Station

nametags (*page 65*), station directions (*page 64*), crayons, markers, paper punch, scissors, yarn, tape, and grocery bags

- Photocopy and cut out the nametags with the bread and cup pictures (*page 65*) for each child and each parent.

- Photocopy the directions for the Who's Who Do-Together Station (*page 64*) and display them in the station.

- Set out the crayons, markers, paper punch, scissors, yarn, tape, and grocery bags.

- Explain to parents that they may set their child's name bag on the floor around the edge of the room. As they complete an activity in the Do-Together Stations, they may put their activity (if it is dry) inside their bags.

Storybook Station

"A Special Meal With Friends" story (*page 41*), Bible; rug, quilt, pillows or rocking chair, station directions (*page 66*)

- Photocopy the story "A Special Meal With Friends" (*page 41*). Set the story and a Bible on a rug or quilt. Add pillows. Or set a rocking chair or other comfortable chair for parents and children to sit in together.

- Photocopy the directions for the Storybook Do-Together Station (*page 66*) and display them in the station.

Mix 'n Match Station

Communion Book pages (*pages 54 and 55*), scissors, station directions (*page 66*)

- Photocopy and cut apart two sets of the Communion Book pages (*pages 54 and 55*) to use as matching cards. Place the pictures on the table or on the rug.

- Photocopy the directions for the Mix 'n Match Do-Together Station (*page 66*) and display them in the station.

Discovery Station

plastic grapes, Communion cups, paper cup, white felt, loaf of bread, bottle of grape juice, Communion items used in your church, station directions (*page 67*)

- Display the plastic grapes, Communion cups, paper cup, white felt, loaf of bread, bottle of grape juice, and the Communion items on a table.

- Photocopy the directions for the Discovery Do-Together Station (*page 67*) and display them in the station.

Place Mat Station

newspapers, construction paper, crayons, paper towels, shallow trays, purple tempera paint, smocks, station directions (*page 67*)

- Cover the table with newspapers.

- Set out construction paper, crayons, and smocks.

- Make paint pads by placing a paper towel in a shallow tray. Pour purple tempera paint on the paper towel.

- Photocopy the directions for the **Place Mat Do-Together Station** (*page 67*) and display them in the station.

Supper Scene Station

scissors, egg cartons, craft sticks, crayons or markers, yarn, glue, tape, supper scene (*page 69*), station directions (*page 68*)

- Photocopy the supper scene (*page 69*) for each child.

- Set out egg cartons, craft sticks, crayons or markers, yarn, glue, and tape.

- Photocopy the directions for the **Supper Scene Do-Together Station** (*page 68*) and display them in the station.

Purple Prints Station

newspapers, Communion cups, purple paint, shallow trays, construction paper, paper towels, smocks, station directions (*page 70*)

- Cover the table with newspapers. Set out construction paper and several Communion cups.

- Pour purple paint into shallow trays.

- Have paint smocks and paper towels available.

- Photocopy the directions for the **Purple Prints Station** (*page 70*) and display them in the station.

Bread Station

ingredients for bread dough, flour, mixing bowl, spoon, measuring cups and spoons, baking sheets, smocks or aprons, station directions (*page 70*)

- You may want to set this station in the kitchen.

- Prepare the bread dough according to the recipe on page 61.

- Set out the smocks or aprons and baking sheets.

- Photocopy the directions for the **Bread Do-Together Station** (*page 70*) and display them in the station.

- Have parents and children make the bread according to the directions. Have a teacher (or other volunteer) bake the bread during the Remember 'n Sing, Sign 'n Tell Bible Story, Bible Verse Find, and Sing-a-Round activities.

Communion Bread

¾ cup butter
¾ cup sugar
¼ teaspoon salt
1 cup sour milk or add 1 tablespoon vinegar
    to 1 cup milk
¼ teaspoon baking soda
1 teaspoon baking powder
4 cups all-purpose flour
flour for kneading

Preheat oven to 350 degrees. Cream butter and sugar together. Add remaining ingredients in the order listed. Mix well. Give each child a golf ball-size piece of dough. Let the children shape the dough into flat loaves on a floured surface. Place each loaf on a baking sheet. Bake at 350 degrees for ten to fifteen minutes. Let cool before eating. Makes 24 to 28 small loaves.

Clean Up

 CD, CD player, *page 72*

- Play "The Cleanup Song" (*page 72*) on the **CD** to signal cleanup time.

Remember 'n Sing

 none

- Have the children and parents hold hands and stand in a circle.

- **Say: Jesus shared bread and juice with his friends at the special meal. When Jesus shared the bread and juice, he asked his friends to remember him. Let's remember Jesus.**

- Sing the song to the tune of "The Farmer in the Dell." Have the children and their parents walk around the circle as you sing together.

> Oh, we remember Jesus.
> Oh, we remember Jesus.
> Jesus shared a special meal.
> Oh, we remember Jesus.

- Stop walking and **say: I remember that Jesus is God's son.**

- Sing the next stanza of the song. Have everyone drop hands and do the suggested motions.

> Oh, Jesus is God's son.
> (*Put hands over heart.*)
> Oh, Jesus is God's son.
> (*Put hands over heart.*)
> We remember our friend Jesus.
> (*Turn around.*)
> Oh, Jesus is God's son.
> (*Put hands over heart.*)

- Sing the first stanza of the song again. Have everyone hold hands and walk around the circle.

- Stop and **say: I remember Jesus loved the children.**

- Sing the next stanza of the song. Have everyone drop hands and do the suggested motions.

> Oh, Jesus loved the children.
> (*Hug self.*)
> Oh, Jesus loved the children.
> (*Hug self.*)
> We remember our friend Jesus.
> (*Turn around.*)
> Oh, Jesus loved the children.
> (*Hug self.*)

- Sing the first stanza of the song a third time. Have everyone hold hands and walk around the circle.

Sign 'n Tell Bible Story

 "We Remember Jesus" story (*page 58*)

- Invite the children to bring their parents and to join you in your story area.

- **Say: Our Bible story today is about the time when Jesus shared a special meal with his friends. I want you to help me tell the Bible story. Each time I say, "We remember Jesus," I want you to sign the words and say the words with me.**

- Teach the children and their parents the signs for "We remember Jesus." The signs are pictured on page 58.

- Tell the story "We Remember Jesus" (*page 58*) using the signs.

Bible Verse Find

plastic grapes, Bible

- Have the children and their parents sit down. Choose a child to hold the Bible open to Luke 22:19.

- **Say: Jesus shared bread and juice with his friends at a special meal. When Jesus shared the bread and juice, he asked his friends to remember him. Jesus said, "Do this in memory of me" (Luke 22:19, *Good News Bible*).**

- Have the children and their parents repeat the verse with you. Show the plastic grapes.

- **Say: The juice Jesus shared at the special meal came from grapes. Grapes can help us remember the special meal.**

- Choose one child to be "it." Have the child put a hand over his or her eyes. Hide the grapes somewhere in your room.

- Have the child uncover her or his eyes. Let the child search the room to find the grapes. When the child is close to the grapes, have the other children and parents clap their hands. When the child moves away from the grapes, have the other children and parents fold their hands in their laps.

- When the child finds the grapes, have the child bring the grapes and stand in front of the other children. Say the Bible verse for the child. Have the child repeat the Bible verse after you.

- Have the child sit down. Continue the game until every child has had an opportunity to find the grapes and repeat the Bible verse.

Sing-a-Round

CD, CD player, plastic grapes

- Have the children and their parents sit in a circle. Sing together the song "A Special Meal" from the **CD**. The tune is "Mary Had a Little Lamb."

- On the phrase, "He passed around the juice and bread," pass the plastic grapes around the circle.

A Special Meal

Jesus shared a special meal,
Special meal, special meal.
Jesus shared a special meal
So many years ago.

He passed around the juice and bread,
Juice and bread, juice and bread.
He passed around the juice and bread
So many years ago.

We can share this special meal,
Special meal, special meal.
We can share this special meal
With friends we've come to know.

Words: Tim Edmonds.
© 1996 Cokesbury

Celebrate Communion

name bags, Communion elements, bread the children made

- Invite parents and children to go to the sanctuary to celebrate Communion. Plan to use the bread the children made.

- **Note: Make arrangements with your pastor to serve Communion. If your pastor is not available, do not have Communion. Let your parents and children enjoy a love feast instead (see page 63).**

- If you plan to end the lesson at the sanctuary, have parents and children gather their activities and place them in their name bags. Have parents bring their name bags with them to the sanctuary.

- Or invite parents and children to participate in Celebration Station activities.

Celebration Station

Use the activities on this page if you choose to have parents and children return to the classroom after the celebration of Communion. These activities are designed for fun and fellowship.

Feast Together

 bread the children made or pita bread, grape juice, cheese, grapes, dates, figs (or fig cookies), olives, pomegranates, place mats made by children, paper cups, napkins, paper plates, platters

• Invite the children and their parents to a love feast.

• Let the children help set the table. Use the place mats made in the Do-Together Station.

• Set out the bread the children made. Or if you used this bread for Communion, buy pita bread. Add platters of Bible-times foods such as cheese, grapes, dates, olives, and figs or fig cookies. Cut a pomegranate in half so the children and their parents may taste the seeds. Pomegranates are usually available in the produce section of grocery stores.

• Ask parents to pour grape juice for themselves and their children.

• Say: **We are tasting foods like Jesus and his friends ate in Bible times. When Jesus shared bread and juice with his friends, he asked them to remember him. Let's remember Jesus while we eat our meal together.**

• Pray: **Thank you, God, for Jesus. Amen.**

Memory Circle

 plastic grapes

• Encourage the children to clean up after the feast.

• Have the children and parents stay seated around the table.

• Pass the plastic grapes to the person sitting next to you and say the Bible verse: "Do this in memory of me" (Luke 22:19, *Good News Bible*).

• Have that person pass the plastic grapes to the person sitting next to him or her and repeat the Bible verse. Continue passing the grapes around the circle until everyone has repeated the Bible verse.

Guess Who?

 none

• Say: **Our church has a special meal to remember Jesus. The special meal is called Communion. Everyone is welcome to eat the bread and drink the juice at Communion. Everyone can remember Jesus.**

• Say: **I'm thinking of someone who can remember Jesus. I'm thinking of someone who . . .**

• Describe something about a child or a parent in the group. You might say things like, "I'm thinking of someone who is wearing a red shirt," or "I'm thinking of someone who has brown hair and blue eyes." Continue with your descriptions until the group guesses the person you are describing.

• Say: **(*Person's name*) is welcome to eat bread and drink juice and remember Jesus.**

• Continue the game until you have described each person.

• Lead the children and their parents in signing "We remember Jesus" (see page 58).

• Have parents and children gather their activities and place them inside their name bags to take home.

Who's Who Station

- Help your child make a nametag and make a nametag for yourself.

- Color the nametags with crayons.

- Write the names on the nametags with a marker.

- Use a paper punch to make a hole in the top of the nametag. Measure a length of yarn to fit easily over your child's head. Thread the yarn through the hole and tie the ends of the yarn together to make a nametag necklace. Or tape the nametags to clothing.

- Give your child a paper bag.

- Let your child decorate the bags with crayons or markers.

- Write your child's name on the bag.

- Open the bag and place it along the wall on the floor. Use the bag to store the things you and your child make at each Do-Together Station.

Talk Together

- **Say: The picture on our nametags shows a loaf of bread and a cup. The picture makes me think about a special meal that Jesus ate with his friends. Jesus shared bread and juice with his friends at the special meal. When Jesus shared the bread and juice, he asked his friends to remember him.**

  - Talk with your child about what she or he remembers about Jesus. Help your child remember the stories of Jesus' birth, Jesus and the children, and Jesus' baptism.

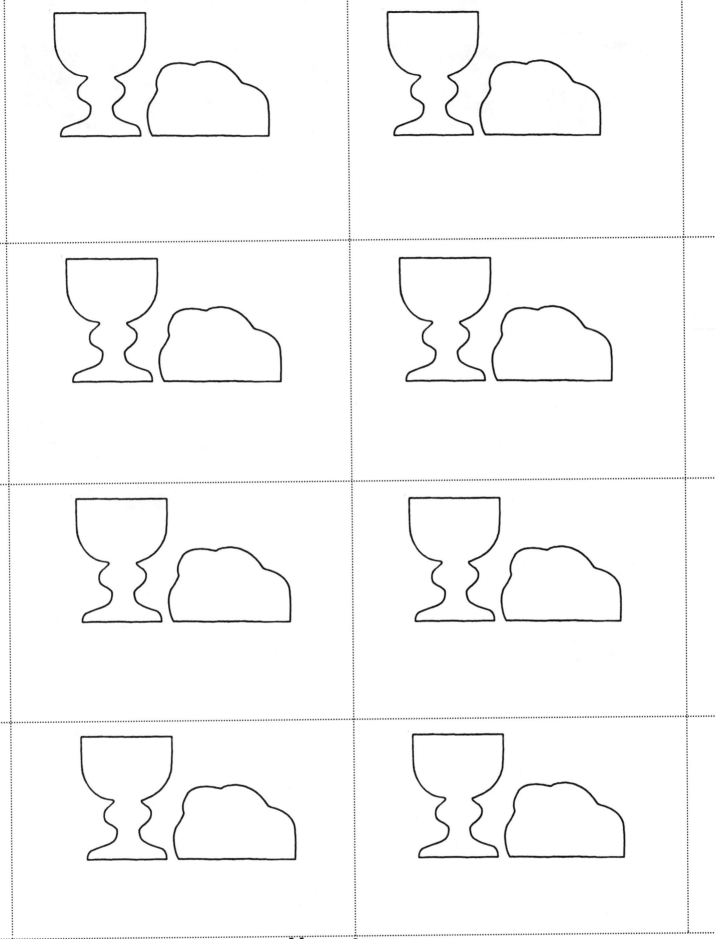

Nametags

65

Storybook Station

- Read the story "A Special Meal With Friends" with your child. When you finish the story, open the Bible to Luke 22:19.

Talk Together

- **Say: The story of the special meal Jesus shared with his friends is in the Bible.**

- Say the Bible verse, "Do this in memory of me" (Luke 22:19, *Good News Bible*).

Mix 'n Match Station

- Place the Communion book pictures on the table or on the rug. Encourage the children to find the matching pictures.

Talk Together

- **Say: Jesus ate a special meal with his friends. Jesus shared bread and juice with his friends at the meal and asked his friends to remember him. We have a special meal in church to remember Jesus. We call the special meal Communion.**

From Touch the Water, Taste the Bread, Ages 3-5. © 1998 Cokesbury. Art © 1994 Cokesbury. Reprinted by permission.

Discovery Station

- Show your child the Communion items. Please touch!

Talk Together

- Talk about how each item is used in Communion. (*We drink juice from the cups; we place bread to eat in the baskets; we cover the bread and juice with the cloth.*)

- Say: Jesus shared bread and juice with his friends at a special meal. When Jesus shared the bread and juice, he asked his friends to remember him. We have a special meal in church to remember Jesus. We call the special meal Communion. We eat bread and drink juice at Communion.

Place Mat Station

- Have your child wear a smock to protect clothing.

- Give your child a piece of construction paper.

- Have your child place a hand with fingers and thumb together on the construction paper. Use a crayon to trace around your child's hand. Use a green crayon to draw leaves and a stem at the top of the palm.

- Show your child how to make thumb prints to represent grapes by pressing a thumb on the purple paint pad and then inside the hand-print. Encourage your child to fill the handprint with grapes.

- Wash hands.

Talk Together

- Say: Jesus shared bread and juice with his friends at a special meal. The juice came from grapes. Grapes can help us remember the special meal.

From *Touch the Water, Taste the Bread, Ages 3-5.* © 1998 Cokesbury. Reprinted by permission.

Supper Scene Station

- Cut the bottom of each egg carton in half lengthwise.

- Turn the strips upside down so the rounded part faces up.

- Cut out the twelve faces and the Jesus figure.

- Let your child decorate the faces with crayons or markers.

- Cut yarn into short pieces. Let your child glue the yarn onto the faces to make hair and beards. The faces will represent the twelve disciples.

- Show your child how to glue each of the twelve faces onto a craft stick.

- Stick each disciple figure into the center of one of the egg cups.

- Give your child the Jesus figure. Have your child decorate the figure with crayons or markers. Let your child glue on pieces of yarn to make hair and a beard.

- Roll the robe of the Jesus figure into a cone. Tape or glue the edges together.

- Stand the Jesus figure between the two "tables of disciples."

Talk Together

- Remind your child that Jesus shared bread and juice with his friends at a special meal. When Jesus shared the bread and juice, he asked his friends to remember him.

- **Say: Our Bible tells us that Jesus asked his friends to "do this in memory of me" (Luke 22:19, *Good News Bible*).**

- Encourage your child to repeat the Bible verse.

Supper Scene Pattern

From *Touch the Water, Taste the Bread, Ages 3–5.* © 1998 Cokesbury. Reprinted by permission.

69

Purple Prints Station

- Have your child wear a smock to protect clothing. Give your child a piece of construction paper and a Communion cup.

- Show your child how to press the rim of the cup into the paint and then onto the construction paper. Let your child cover the paper with prints.

Talk Together

- **Say: Our church has a special meal called Communion to remember Jesus. At Communion we eat bread and drink juice and remember Jesus. Sometimes we drink juice from small cups like these Communion cups.**

- Talk with your child about the way your church serves Communion.

Bread Station

- Lightly flour the work surface. Give your child a golf ball-size piece of bread dough.

- Let your child shape the dough into a flat loaf on the floured surface. Place the loaf on the baking sheet.

- Let your child know that you will eat the bread later.

Talk Together

- **Say: Jesus told his friends to remember him when they ate bread and drank juice. Jesus told his friends to "do this in memory of me" (Luke 22:19, *Good News Bible*).**

- Encourage your child to repeat the Bible verse.

- **Say: Our church has a special meal when we eat bread and drink juice and remember Jesus. The special meal is called Communion.**

From *Touch the Water, Taste the Bread, Ages 3-5.* © 1998 Cokesbury. Reprinted by permission.

Parents

You are invited to "Parents and Children Learning Together About Communion"

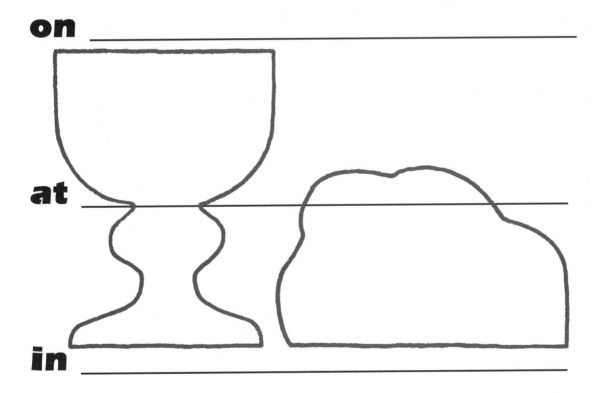

on _____

at _____

in _____

Enjoy "Do-Together" Stations that will help you talk with your child about the sacrament of Communion.

The Cleanup Song

WORDS and MUSIC: John D. Horman
© 2000 Cokesbury